Mnen
Meth

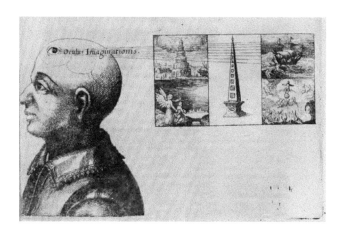

Mnemonic Methods

ROBERT FLUDD
ON THE
ART OF MEMORY

from

Utriusque cosmi maioris scilicet et minoris metaphysica,
physica atque technica Historia

*(The metaphysical, physical, and technical history of the two
worlds, namely the greater and the lesser) of 1617-1621*

Lewis Masonic

First published 2020

ISBN 978 0 85318 591 8

Published by Lewis Masonic

an imprint of Ian Allan Publishing Ltd, Shepperton, Middx TW17 8AS.
Printed in England.

Visit the Lewis Masonic website at www.lewismasonic.co.uk

Picture Credits
Every effort has been made to identify and correctly attribute photographic credits. Should any error have occurred this is entirely unintentional.

Cover image: Courtesy of Paul Ferguson

Contents

FLUDD'S MNEMONIC METHODS:
FROM MEMORY TO MAGIC?

Paul Ferguson

"A deep Philosopher, and great Physician, he was of the Order of the Rosa Crucians, and I must confesse my self ignorant of the first Founder and Sanctions thereof, perchance none know it, but those that are of it. Sure I am, that a Rose is the sweetest of Flowers, and a Cross accounted the sacredest of forms or figures, so that much of eminency must be imported in their composition."

From Dr. Thomas Fuller's biography of Fludd in his *History of the Worthies of England* (1662).

I – Beginnings

Robert Fludd (or Flud, or Floid, or Flood or – as he himself liked to style himself with his elegant Latinity – Robertus de Fluctibus) was born in 1574 at Milgate House in the Kent village of Bearsted near Maidstone. His family seems to have been of Welsh origin. His father, Sir Thomas, was a man of substance, a Member of Parliament and, amongst other things, Treasurer of the Cinque Ports.

Robert's early years are obscure, but we know that he spent the 1590s studying at St. John's College, Oxford (BA 1597, MA 1598). Over the next few years he toured the Continent, studying a hodgepodge of subjects both mainstream and esoteric, and earning his living as an itinerant teacher of mathematics and mnemonics to young aristocrats.

At some point he decided to study medicine, and graduated from Christ Church, Oxford as MB (1604) and MD (1605). But practising medicine required registration with the College of Physicians, and Fludd seems to have failed the *viva* six times, on each occasion arguing with the examiners about the shortcomings of traditional Galenic medicine compared with its holistic Paracelsian rival. It is possible that, during his time at St. John's, Fludd had met Matthew Gwinne, the college's Medical Fellow and a keen student of Paracelsian theories. Alternatively, he may have fallen under Paracelsian influence during his time on the Continent. Whatever the case, he eventually stopped arguing and received his licence to practise, establishing a surgery in Fenchurch Street in London.

From even these few biographical details we can construct a portrait of Fludd as a versatile, independent-minded and progressive thinker – if, perhaps, a somewhat stubborn one – and a man destined to make his mark as an encyclopaedist. Indeed, the short treatise on the Art of Memory to be found here forms part of a formidably learned and richly illustrated two-volume work, the *Utriusque Cosmi, Maioris scilicet et Minoris, metaphysica, physica, atque technica Historia* ('The metaphysical, physical, and technical history of the two worlds, namely the greater and the lesser', i.e. the macrocosm and the microcosm), published between 1617 and 1621 in Germany (for purely financial reasons according to Fludd, rather than because he had been accused by the polymath Marin Mersenne and others of dabbling in magic, about which more anon).

Though never completed, these volumes cover not just alchemy, astrology, the Cabbala and divination – all wrapped up within the guiding-thread of all Fludd's work, namely the interrelationship between God, the natural world, and the world of humanity – but also an array of practical subjects, such as mechanics, architecture, fortifications, military tactics, hydrology, musicology (Fludd was a talented composer), mathematics, geometry, optics, drawing, chemistry and, of course, medicine. The work even includes a proposal for a perpetual-motion machine which was still forming the subject of serious experimentation in Victorian times. So, obviously a man to be reckoned with.

II – Fludd's Treatise on Memory: Two Books in One?

The basic assumption behind the present essay is that Fludd's treatise on memory is effectively two books in one: an exoteric text for the budding memory-artist and, intertwined with it, a more esoteric narrative outlining a way in which the memory might be used to achieve a peculiarly Rosicrucian magical goal. In support of this idea, I draw heavily upon the material contained in Chapter X of Manly Palmer Hall's *Man, The Grand Symbol of the Mysteries* and in Chapter XV of *The Art of Memory* by Frances Yates.

I shall ignore those parts of Fludd's treatise which relate purely to conventional mnemonics, and instead focus on what I take to be the esoteric aspects of the text. Nor shall I be discussing Fludd's short treatise on arithmetical memory included as an appendix to this book. Whether it has an esoteric dimension I am not sure: Fludd was a mathematician and teacher of mathematics as well as an esotericist, so it may have served a purely practical purpose. Further research may settle the matter.

There are four main reasons why I think that Fludd's main treatise serves a dual purpose, both exoteric and esoteric:

1. Take the illustration on the first page (fig. 1). In this volume of many pictures, most of them covered in explanatory labels, it is unusual to find imagery so enigmatic. The images have no legends, and are never mentioned again. We shall deal in a moment with the head-and-shoulders profile on the left of the engraving. As for the five images in the right-hand grid (corresponding to that used in Fludd's Square Art – see Chapter XI of the First Book), Frances Yates identifies them as the Tower of Babel; Tobias and the Angel Raphael from the Book of Tobit; a ship at sea; and the Last Judgement.

These images seem to have been produced specifically for the *Utriusque Cosmi*; I have not, for example, been able to identify the obelisk, which is an obvious starting-point for exploring their origin. We must however assume that they have some sort of meaning as, although Fludd often writes at great length, he never includes superfluous material. Frances Yates ingeniously suggests that they might be interpreted to mean that Fludd's little book is actually a hieroglyphic code (the obelisk) leading to the unravelling of human confusion (the Tower of Babel) under angelic guidance (Tobias and Raphael) to guide us through stormy seas (the ship) to religious safety (the Last Judgement), though she herself describes this exegesis as possibly 'over-fanciful'.

The Tobias story is drawn from the semi-apocryphal Book of Tobit, and recounts how the blind Tobit's son Tobias meets 'unawares' the archangel Raphael (Tobit 5:5-6), who then instructs him what to do with a giant fish he has caught (Tobit 6:2-9). This essentially involves gutting it and conserving the parts, including the gall (Tobit 6:8: "As for the gall," says Raphael, "it is good to anoint a man that hath whiteness in his eyes, and he shall be healed."). Later (Tobit 11:11-14) Tobias does indeed restore his father's eyesight with the gall: "...and he strake of the gall on his father's eyes, saying, Be of good hope, my father./And when his eyes began to smart, he rubbed them;/And the whiteness pilled [sic] away from the corners of his eyes: and when he saw his son, he fell upon his neck./And he wept, and said, Blessed art thou, O God, and blessed is thy name for ever; and blessed are all thine holy angels."

So here we have what I suspect is a reference to the development of clairvoyance or, at least, to a heightened insight into the material and spiritual worlds (using the *oculus imaginationis*, the 'eye of the imagination' shown in the left-hand image) as the scales fall from our eyes using the 'gall' of, among other possibilities, a memory-system. We also have a reference to human contact with the superhuman, in this case the Archangel Raphael.

I find the other four images harder to interpret. We know that in 1619 the alleged founder of the Rosicrucian Brotherhood, Johann Valentin Andreae, published a short work entitled *Turris Babel* ('Tower of Babel)', essentially informing the world, presumably completely disingenuously, that the Rosicrucians did not exist. This image may therefore be a reference to Fludd's rumoured membership of that order.

The ship image might be a pun on the author's name, *de Fluctibus*, or it may represent the Hebrew character *sin* or *shin* (ש) which, according to Hargrave Jennings (*The Rosicrucians*, p. 52) is "full of secret important meanings", though unfortunately he does not tell us

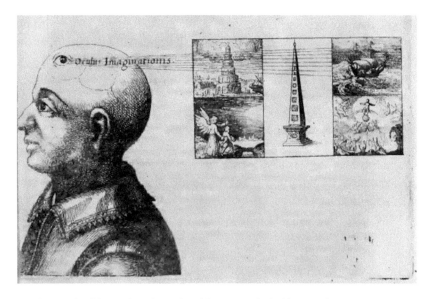

Fig. 1. The illustration from the title-page of Fludd's treatise on memory.

what they are. Below I cast doubt on whether Giordano Bruno ever directly influenced Fludd, but Bruno's *La Cena de le Ceneri (The Ash Wednesday Supper)* of 1584 contains a famous engraving of a ship at sea to accompany a discussion anticipating Galileo's relativity principle. Coincidence? It may also refer to the ship of Scottish hero William Wallace, which was hauled from the bottom of the Tay under the supervision of esotericist and memory-expert Alexander Dicsone[1] (1558-1604), a disciple of Giordano Bruno and a near-contemporary of Fludd, whose works we have recently made available as *The Hermetic Art of Memory.*

As for the image at the bottom-right, which Frances Yates interprets as the Last Judgement, it looks to me more like Christ trailing clouds of glory, but it could also depict the exalted state of the illumined Initiate, with the arms representing a cross and the globe arguably the heart of a rose. As for the obelisk, as I said above I have not been able to trace it to any particular original or even pattern. Suffice it to say that the obelisk is one of the great Christianised Hermetic symbols. Hargrave Jennings informs us, not I suspect entirely accurately, that "There is an obelisk, altered to suit Christian ideas (and surmounted in most instances in modern times by a cross), in front of every church in Rome. There are few churchyards in England without a phallus or obelisk. On the top is usually now fixed a dial. In former times, when the obeliscar form was adopted for ornaments of all sorts, it was one of the various kinds of Christian-acceptable cross which was placed on the summit" (Jennings, *The Rosicrucians*, p. 148). Not an inappropriate image therefore for a book by someone who worked under strong Hermetic influences while remaining a devout Anglican to the end of his life. It seems to be telling us that Hermeticism was a foreshadowing of Christianity, and is in no way an enemy of it.

Finally, we have the image of the man on the left of the illustration. We note that the skull is marked with three circles, presumably corresponding to the three areas of the brain we shall consider in more detail below when we come to examine the ventricular theory. This theory is unfortunately riddled with misunderstandings and terminological confusion, though the great Italian anatomists of the Renaissance brought some rational order to it. Suffice it to say at this point that the traditional paradigm assigned Imagination and the task of gathering visual phenomena to the front of the brain, with Reason allocated to the middle, and Memory to the rear.

Fludd's illustration follows this model, with the 'eye of the imagination' (the *oculus imaginationis*) at the front. This is presumably a reference to the pineal gland or 'third eye'. Fludd's near-contemporary René Descartes was known to have a keen interest in this structure, but those of his works that mention it (*Les Passions de l'âme* of 1649 and *L'Homme*, written before 1637 but only published more than a decade after his death in 1650) all post-date Fludd's volume. In any case, Descartes seemed to have had eccentric ideas about the pineal gland's location, so we can perhaps discount any Cartesian influence on Fludd in this regard. Since a cone of rays is shown sweeping backwards from it through the whole of the skull, an alternative interpretation might be that the 'eye of the imagination' is a single all-encompassing structure or system whose development and integration is the task of the student of the treatise that follows.

2. For someone who usually writes so lucidly, logically and economically, Fludd's treatise on memory is curiously disjointed and obscure. In fact, it reads like the truncated remains of a longer work. Chapter IX of the First Book in particular sticks out like a sore thumb, with its Cabbalistic reference to the sphere of fire. Perhaps, in view of the allegations of sorcery that Fludd was facing, he felt it sensible to omit themes that might provide ammunition to his enemies. Fludd's habit of jumping backwards and forwards between the Square Art and the Round Art does not help, and some passages are wilfully obscure.

We know that the texts of Giordano Bruno[2], a mnemonicist who made no secret of the esoteric sources of his inspiration, are amplified with incantations to Circe which flesh them out and give them a more satisfying structure, and Fludd may have omitted material of a similar character. I should state at this point that I do not think Bruno directly influenced Fludd. Bruno was a Catholic turned pagan, Fludd a steadfast Anglican who came under early Catholic influences but was not persuaded by them; Bruno was a revolutionary, Fludd a traditionalist; Bruno was a priest, Fludd a physician; Bruno had the Latin temperament, Fludd was a Celt and a natural mystic. There may be some similarities in thinking and techniques, but I would say these were almost certainly the result of coincidence. Yet it may still have been Fludd's intention that his text be supplemented with incantatory material similar to Bruno's Circe verses. Passages from the Book of Tobit perhaps or, given the subject-matter of Chapter VI of the Second Book, texts relating to Jason, Medea and the Golden Fleece taken from the Greek *Argonautica* of Apollonius of Rhodes or the Latin of Valerius Flaccus?

3. Fludd makes two clear distinctions that serve to divide his subject into a 'lower', more accessible and practical mnemonic technique, and a 'higher' one aimed at esotericists.

First, there is the important distinction between 'natural' and 'artificial' memory (Chapters 2 to 4 of the First Book). In the former, which is achieved through conventional physiological processes, there is no magical aspect, whereas in the latter (which may be physiologically quite different, as we shall see below) the imagination is used to 'swallow' target-images and internalise them. Though artificial memory 'piggy-backs' on natural memory, and cannot function without it, it greatly transcends it.

Second, there is Fludd's distinction between the Square or Quadrate System, concerned with corporeal objects and aimed at the astronomically unsophisticated, and the more challenging Round System (Chapter 5 of the First Book), devoted to ideal forms and transcending earthly limitations to embrace the planets in both their astronomical and astrological aspects. The Round Art makes explicit use of decanic images (Chapter IV of the Second Book) similar to those used by Bruno (See Yates, *The Art of Memory*, Chapter IX).

At this point I should admit that I take comfort from Frances Yates's complete inability to explain how Bruno's or Fludd's magical systems actually worked. Below I suggest how Fludd's system might have been used in practice, although there is much further work to be done. But back to my reasons for thinking that this can be seen as a magical treatise.

4. We have a plate (fig. 2) from the title-page of part II.I.II of the *Utriusque Cosmi* – a section devoted to what Fludd called the 'technical history of the Microcosm' – which shows how he located the Art of Memory within his encyclopaedic programme as one of seven 'esoteric' arts.

In his dispute with the small-fry clergyman William Foster, who had accused him of being a sorcerer, Fludd had explained his reasons for including this section in the *Utriusque Cosmi*, saying that he wished to:

"...write as well the naturall discoverie of the great world, and the little world, which we call man, as well as to touch by way of an Encyclophy [encyclopaedia] or Epitome of all arts, as well lawful, which I did commend, as those which are esteemed unlawfull, which I did utterly condemne as superstitious, and of little or no probabilitie at all; among the rest, where I came to speake of the Arts which belong unto the little world or man, I mention the Science of Genethlialogie, which treateth of the Judgement of Nativities, wherein I produce the great dispute between the two famous philosophers, Porphyrie and Iamblicus, whereof the first did hold that a man might come to the knowledge of his owne Genius or good Angell by the art of astrologie… Iamblicus his opinion was that a man had neede of the assistance and knowledge of a higher spirit than was any of those which were Governours of Fatalitie… I seemed there to consent with Iamblicus, averring with him, that without the revelation of that high and heavenly Spirit, which was granted unto the Elect, none could come to the familiaritie or knowledge of his good Angell." (original spelling retained)

(By 'unlawful' arts Fludd probably meant those that claimed to predict the future.)

In Chapter I of the First Book of the *Utriusque Cosmi*, Fludd tells us that he delved into the more recondite aspects of mnemonics (*hujus scientiæ penetralia*) during his time in Marseilles (*Marcelliis*), and this may have included some esoteric study. I shall stick my neck out and speculate that *Marcelliis* may actually be a coded reference to Marcellus Ficin (better known as Marsilio Ficino), in whose Neoplatonist works Fludd is known to have immersed himself. Later in the First Book, in Chapter IV, Fludd expresses his scepticism about the use of ritual magic as a means of acquiring mastery of the art of memory. In the light of these two reference I think we can fairly place Fludd in the 'practical mystic' category rather than any other. Certainly, his support for Iamblichus in the quotation above suggests a leaning towards theurgy rather than towards the more intellectual Neoplatonism of many of his English contemporaries. But that Fludd had certainly dabbled in natural magic of the non-ritualistic variety is suggested by a passage in J. B. Craven's biography, where Craven refers to the third part of Fludd's earliest publication, the *Apologia Compendiaria* of 1616, and subsequently quotes from it:

"Natural magic is that secret and hidden part of nature-studies in which the mystical and secret properties of all natural things are sought after; so, therefore, the royal wise men, who, by the leading of the new star in the east, sought the new-born Christ, were called the magi, because they

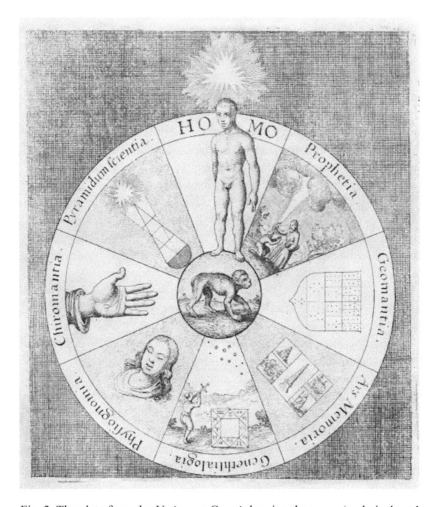

Fig. 2. The plate from the *Utriusque Cosmi* showing the seven 'technical arts' that Fludd assigned to a separate section of his text, namely Prophecy, Geomancy, the Art of Memory, Astrology, Physiognomy, Palmistry and the Science of Pyramids. In the centre is the Ape of Nature, which seems to have been Fludd's favourite symbol for the intellectually-curious aspect of the human being, while the man above it, crowned with a 'glory', seems to have been given a deliberately childlike appearance.

had attained the highest nature-knowledge of both heavenly and earthly things. In this same knowledge Solomon was well advanced, for he knew the secret powers and properties of all things. Again, those who have divined the secrets of mathematical magic have performed astonishing things. Such were the wooden flying doves of Archetas, the metal speaking heads of Roger Bacon and Albertus Magnus. Fludd adds, 'I have also myself, by diligence in this art, prepared a wooden ox, which, like a natural ox, alternately moves and roars; a dragon, moving its wings and hissing, which spits out of its jaws fire and flames against the ox; a lyre, which, of its own motive, plays a symphony and many other things, about which I must confess that they cannot be done by mere mathematics without the co-operation of natural magic'."

I think I have shown that there is an esoteric dimension to this little text which is worth exploring, and that we can locate Fludd within an occult mnemonic tradition that resembles that of Giordano Bruno but is not of a piece with it. It might help, before we examine the esoteric aspect more closely, to trace the intellectual tradition behind Fludd's conception of memory. This is not a very difficult task as, in general, it was a very conservative and consistent one.

III – The Intellectual Background: the Ventricular Theory

Western theories on memory can be traced back – as, I suppose, can most Western scientific speculation – to Aristotle. His *ventricular theory* of brain structure posited the existence of four chambers in the brain: the anterior, which governed common sense, from which the nerves of the five senses branched off, and within which all sensory phenomena were brought together; two wing-shaped middle ventricles, which were the seat of the imagination, judgement and reflection, where the sensory impressions were processed; and the posterior chamber at the back of the head, which was the seat of memory and the location where the impressions processed in the middle ventricles were stored and from which they might be subsequently retrieved with greater or lesser degrees of accuracy and vividness.

Aristotle's ventricular scheme was taken over, with hardly any fresh input or refinement, by a succession of later writers. According to the 5th century anthologist Aetios, two writers from the late 4th century – Posidonius of Byzantium and Nemesius of Emesa – assigned

Imagination to the anterior ventricle, Reason to the middle ventricle, and Memory to the hind part of the brain. This view persisted, with few variants, into the Middle Ages, where writers such as the 11th century Italian physician Pietro Clerico (or Petrocello, the author of the influential *Practica Petrocelli Salernitani*) largely adopted the Aristotelian paradigm, with memory once again allocated to the fourth or posterior ventricle, but with the additional notion that this ventricle was also the seat of the soul, a view later shared by the 17th century English esotericist John Heydon. As we shall see later, Fludd distributed the soul across all the ventricles.

Fig. 3. Part of an illustration from Petrus de Montagnana's *Fasciculus Medicine* of 1491 showing the ventricular assignment of the memory function (*Cellula memorativa*).

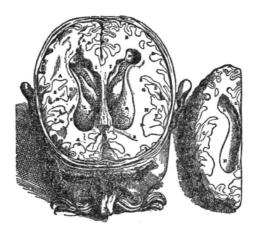

Fig. 4. An illustration from Vesalius showing the middle ventricles as L and M.

Bernard (de) Gordon, a Scottish physician and a professor at the University of Montpelier, in his *Affectus praeternaturam curandi Methodus* written in 1296, also adopted the Aristotelian scheme, but to the four traditional structures, which he claimed are susceptible to corruption and deterioration, he assigned a higher, divine and incorruptible faculty, which he called the 'Intellect', which in his system has no structure of its own but uses the four ventricles as media for acting upon the external world. Even later works, such as Petrus de Montagnana's *Fasciculus Medicinae* of 1491 (fig. 3), the *De Humani Corporis Fabrica* (1543) of the great Flemish anatomist Andreas Vesalius (fig. 4), and the 1562 work on memory by the Venetian Lodovico Dolce entitled *Dialogo di M. Lodovico Dolce, nel quale si ragiona del modo di accrescere, & conservar la Memoria* ('Signor Dolce's dialogue on how to increase and conserve the memory') accept the traditional Aristotelian ventricular format without serious challenge.

It will be appreciated that the ventricles are not so much organs as *spaces*, and this raises the question of what it is that operates within the spaces to bring about the various phenomena such as the formation and retention of images that go to make up the memory-process. Early medical writers such as those mentioned above (including Vesalius) posited a rather underpowered theory of 'animal spirits' to explain brain-activity. Here is Vesalius, in his *De Humani Corporis Fabrica*, explaining how the ventricles work:

"The air we breathe penetrates the cribriform [mesh-shaped] process of the ethmoidal bone and passes through the Eustachian tubes where it is rarefied to make it acceptable to the brain before insinuating the first and second ventricles, where it is formed into animal spirits. These then pass into the third ventricle of the brain, and thence into the ventricle of the cerebellum. From this ventricle a considerable amount of the animal spirits is transmitted into the *medulla oblongata* and the nerves propagated from it. The other portion of the spirits is used for the divine operations of the original soul and is likewise transmitted from the ventricle of the brain to the nerves of sense and motion."

In fact, the Venetian anatomist Niccolò Massa had shown as early as 1536 that the ventricles were actually filled with a fluid instead of either nothing at all or the mysterious psychic *pneuma* or animal spirits originally posited by Galen. We shall return to that fluid later.

Running largely in parallel with the ideas of the physicians and anatomists were the systems of the great philosophers and theologians of the Middle Ages, such as Thomas Aquinas and Albertus Magnus (fig. 5), who had also been heavily influenced by Aristotle and who, having divided the mind into parts that corresponded to the imagination, ratiocination, cogitation and memory, then proceeded to divide the brain along similar lines. Vesalius, in his commentary confirming the location of the memory in the posterior ventricle, refers to the theologians, mentioning their belief that a vermiform (worm-shaped) process served as a channel whereby the "phantoms of the mind" could pass into the cerebellum where the memory has its seat. This worm-shaped process plays an important part in Fludd's memory system, as we shall see.

Another probable influence on Fludd's thinking was Gregorius Reisch (fig. 6), whose encyclopaedia for young people, the *Margarita*

Fig. 5. The ventricles as the seat of the Soul, according to the theologian Albertus Magnus, with the 'III Ventriculus' at the back of the head as the seat of memory.

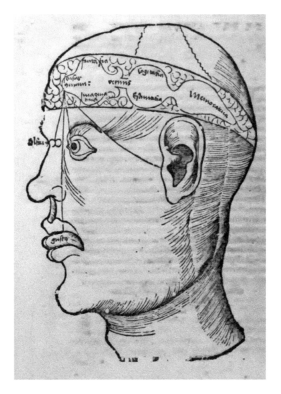

Fig. 6. An illustration from Gregor Reisch's *Margarita Philosophica*,
with the memory function (*memorativa*) assigned to its traditional place
at the back of the head. The vermiform (worm-like) process (*vermis*)
is also shown.

Philosophica of 1583, may even have given Fludd the idea for his own
magnum opus.

Unfortunately, from a terminological perspective, things were not so
straightforward as they might appear at first glance. For one thing, many
mediaeval writings on the subject display a particular confusion between
the pineal gland and the vermiform (worm-shaped) structure in the
cerebellum to which the theologians and Vesalius referred. Galen had
believed that this latter structure was the true regulator of the psychic
pneuma ('animal spirits') flowing between the middle and posterior
ventricles, and had combined this with the ventricular localisation
doctrine dating back, as we have seen, to Aristotle. Examples of the latter
'combined theory' include the text *On the difference between spirit and
soul* by the Melkite physician Qusta ibn Luqa (or Costa ben Luca, 864-

923 AD) in which he says that people who want to remember something should look upwards, thus raising the vermiform appendage and allowing for memory-retrieval from the posterior ventricle. Anyone who has seen someone struggling to remember something will be able to confirm the correctness of this observation.

Further terminological confusion was caused by the use of the term *pinea* to describe the vermiform structure by the encyclopaedist Vincent of Beauvais in the 13th century and by Jacobus Publicius in 1492, while in 1306 Mondino dei Luzzi seems to have come much nearer the mark by describing the choroid plexus as "a blood-red substance similar to a long worm, which opens and closes the canal between the anterior and middle ventricles".

By the late Middle Ages therefore there were three 'worms' competing for the honour of being the effective channel for the memory: the vermis of the cerebellum, the choroid plexus, and the pineal gland. From Mondino's description I think we can conclude that the vermiform structure mentioned by Fludd and others is indeed the choroid plexus, which Fludd correctly locates between the anterior and middle ventricles. This structure is formed by the *tela choroidea* (or *tela chorioidea*), defined anatomically as a region of meningeal *pia mater* which adheres to the underlying ependyma and gives rise to the choroid plexus in each of the brain's four ventricles.

As Fludd himself explains, in Chapter III of the First Book:

"When the imagination presents fictitious images to the channel that contains the vermiform process the latter introduces them, by its extension, into that chamber of the brain where the reasoning faculty is located, where they can be carefully and rationally assessed. From there they are sent immediately to the memory-chamber so that, within the pit of that chamber, they can be captured and stored there by the self-contraction of the vermiform process."

Very much in passing, we should also note that if we add to these four ventricles the fifth (terminal) ventricle (known as the ventricle of Krause), the tiny tube to be found in the spinal cord as a sixth ventricle, and the skull itself as an all-encompassing seventh, then we have the seven brain-cavities described by Helena Blavatsky and other occultists, all "filled with Akasha, each cavity having its own colour, according to the state of consciousness" (Collected Writings vol. XII (Wheaton: Theosophical Publishing House, 1980), p. 618, as well as the seven 'caves' of the remarkable mediaeval seer St. Hildegard of Bingen:

"From the summit of the vessel of the brain to the extremity of the forehead seven equal spaces can be distinguished. Here the seven planets are designated, the uppermost planet in the highest part, the Sun in the middle, and the other planets distributed among the other places." (Charles Singer, 'Scientific Views and Visions of St. Hildegard', in *Studies in the History of Method of Science*, vol I, Oxford 1917).

St. Hildegard's ideas of planetary correspondences for the brain are occasionally depicted in contemporary art, suggesting a wider dissemination of her ideas (fig. 7).

To end this section, I quote a passage from Chapter X of Manly Palmer Hall's *Man, The Grand Symbol of the Mysteries*, which may shed some light on the esoteric potential of Fludd's memory-system:

"There are delicate fringelike processes consisting almost entirely of blood vessels which project into the third, fourth, and lateral ventricles of the brain and are termed the choroid plexuses. It is the epithelial cells of these plexuses that secrete the cerebrospinal fluid and pour it into the

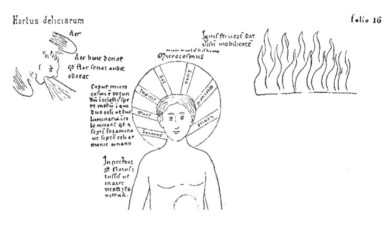

Fig. 7. Part of an illustration from the *Hortus deliciarum* of Abbess Herrad of Landsberg (c. 1130-195) showing planetary correspondences with the brain (after Straub & Keller's reproduction).

ventricles, from whence it flows through the numerous apertures which open into the subarachnoid spaces. Santee describes the cerebrospinal fluid which fills the various serous spaces of the central nervous system as a displaceable fluid "more like tears and sweat than lymph" in consistency. In writing of the *Brahmarandhra* as the greatest of the chambers in the brain, Dr. Rele says that this cavity is constantly secreting a fluid called "the nectar of life" or "the divine fluid," which bathes the brain and the spinal cord. The cerebrospinal fluid, then, is synonymous with the "tears of the sky God," or "the wine-weeping heavens," yes, even *lachrymae Christi*, "the tears of Christ.".... In their search for the elixir of life, the alchemists discovered the occult properties of a certain mysterious "dew" and were moved to write thereof, but always in a most guarded manner. In the preparation of their medicines with which they sought to heal all the diseases and evils of the world, these philosophers made use of a crystalline "dew" gathered at night on plates of glass during the major conjunctions of planets and at certain phases of the moon. They declared that they were thus able to capture the celestial "virtues" and apply them to the all too numerous ills of humankind. ... Several authors, including Mosheim and Higgins, arc of the opinion that the word Rosicrucian is derived from the words *Ros* and *crux*. *Ros* is a Latin word which may be translated dew or dripping moisture or even tears without taxing the credulity. In a Gnostic ritual it is written that the rulers of the sphere (zodiac) create the soul from their own substance " out of the tears of their eyes and the sweat of their torment." The Latin form of rose is *rosa* and by a simple cabala this becomes *ros*-a. As the first of the sacred vowels the a is the moon, which in the Mysteries was the symbol of the brain, as already noted. In early anatomical treatises it is even mentioned that the brain moves in the skull according to the phases of the moon. So the word can be interpreted as the "dew or moisture from the brain" or, as the Rosicrucians themselves called it, "the dew in the brain." This is the "dew" from heaven described by the sages as "descending upon the tops of he mountains." In their letter to Eugenius Philalethes, the Brothers of R. C. hint at this mystery in these words: "Near the daybreak there shall be a great calm and you shall see the Day-Star arise and the dawning will appear, and you shall perceive a great treasure. The chief thing in it, and the most perfect, is a certain exalted tincture, with which the world (if it served God and were worthy of such gifts) might be tinged and turned into pure gold.".... The philosophers [alchemists] also revealed that this mysterious "dew" drips down into the heart of the redeemed (baptism), by which such a man is empowered to understand all mysteries. Therefore, the "dew" is also called truth. Hence, Emanuel Swedenborg, the uninitiated seer, refers to "dew" in one place as the truth of good, which is derived from a state of innocence and peace, and in another place as the multiplication of good from truth and the fructification of good by truth. By the term multiplication it is indicated that Swedenborg sensed the alchemical significance of that heavenly moisture which is both physical and spiritual in its esoteric interpretation… The activity of the human brain, which we have already seen to be filled and surrounded by a subtle humidity, causes an akashic precipitation, a brain "dew," which is more of a luminous ether than a liquid. This "dew," however, is more tangible than a gas, and as the manna is said to have fallen from heaven, so this "dew" of thought trickles down between the two hemispheres of the cerebrum and finally fills the third ventricle, which is the reservoir, so to speak, of this heavenly water. This "dew" carries in suspension, or as the alchemists might say, is "tinctured" by the mental activity of the seven brain stars which form the northern constellation of man. It is this water which is contained within the celestial microcosmic "Dipper," which is called by the Hindus the constellation of the Seven Rishis of the Pole… Having reached the third ventricle and being caught therein, the "dew" must act in conformity with the symbolism involved. It must be caught by the wise man in the cup of the Mysteries. We must, therefore, search for the sacred vessel, the lachrimatory, which is to hold the tears of the brain." (pp. 220-4, 230-1).

IV – Fludd's Conception of the Mind

In a moment we shall look at a diagram from the *Utriusque Cosmi* which seems to draw upon both Cabbalistic and Rosicrucian sources, and which helps us understand Fludd's conception of the mind and the place of memory within it, but first we shall take a very brief look at these influences.

In 1622, the year after the publication of the *Utriusque Cosmi* was completed, the Sorbonne scholar Marin Mersenne published his *Quaestiones Celebres in Genesim*, which contained a furious attack on Fludd, essentially accusing him of atheism and sorcery. Fludd was slow to respond, for his riposte, entitled *Sophiae cum Moria Certamen* ('The duel between wisdom and folly') along with its appendix *Summum Bonum*, did not appear until 1629.

Although Fludd always denied authorship of the latter text, which is essentially a defence of the Rosicrucian Brotherhood, there is little doubt that, at the very least, it was published with his entire knowledge and approval. Whether Fludd was ever a member of the Brotherhood we cannot be sure, but he certainly seems to have endorsed its ideas, and the image on the title-page of the *Summum Bonum* (fig. 8) is justly famous.

As for the Cabbala, the fourth book of Fludd's *Sophiae cum Moria Certamen* is devoted to its. We know for sure that he was a keen student of the works of the Cabbalistic scholars Johann Reuchlin and Giovanni Pico della Mirandola, and there is little doubt that his profound studies

Fig. 8. The famous Rose and Cross image from the *Summum Bonum* with the legend, 'The Rose gives Honey to the Bees'.

of these texts coloured his understanding of how the mind actually functions every bit as much as his Rosicrucian conceptions, as Manly Palmer Hall explains in his *Man, the Grand Symbol of the Mysteries*:

"In his work on Rosicrucian anatomy, the *Microcosmi Historia*, Robert Fludd assigns the three departments of the Empyrean (or mundane heaven) to the cranium of the microcosm (man). In common with Boehme, therefore, he locates the paradisaical spheres in the head, or highest part, of the inferior Adam. Fludd calls the highest plane or division of the brain the Radius of Deity, or the Uncreated Light. The middle he designates the Luminous Sphere, or the Created Light; and the lowest he terms the Spiritual Sphere, or the Empyrean. This classification Fludd derives from the Chaldaic-Cabbalistic concept of *Ain Soph*. The Absolute Deity of The Zohar is caused to assume definition by imposing upon it certain hypothetical qualifications. The first is Boundlessness, the second Boundless Life, and the third Boundless Light. Fludd further visualises these spiritual aspects as abiding in certain recesses of the brain. He establishes the location of these compartments by recourse to the divisions of the cranium laid down by earlier anatomists. In his astronomical teachings, Pythagoras taught that the gods did not reside in the planetary bodies but, more correctly, in the interplanetary 'intervals'. (Iamblichus.) In accordance with this astronomical concept, mediaeval disciples of Galen and Avicenna did not assign organs to the 'spirits' (vital centres) in the brain but instead assigned them cavities (ventricles) in which to mingle their essences. From this viewpoint, the soul was likened to a vapour, gas, or even a humidity, bottled up during life in remote caverns of the body (i.e., the ventricles, arteries, etc.)." (p. 209-210)

In his *Utriusque Cosmi*, Fludd supplies us with a diagram illustrating his conception of how the Macrocosm and Microcosm interacted, and the place of memory within this scheme. We have translated the legends below.

The French writer Gillot de Givry, in his *Musée des Sorciers*, pp. 267-8, interprets Fludd's diagram as follows:

[Elle] montre comment le monde supérieur agit sur le cerveau humain… C'est le monde céleste, composé de Dieu et des anges, qui pénètre

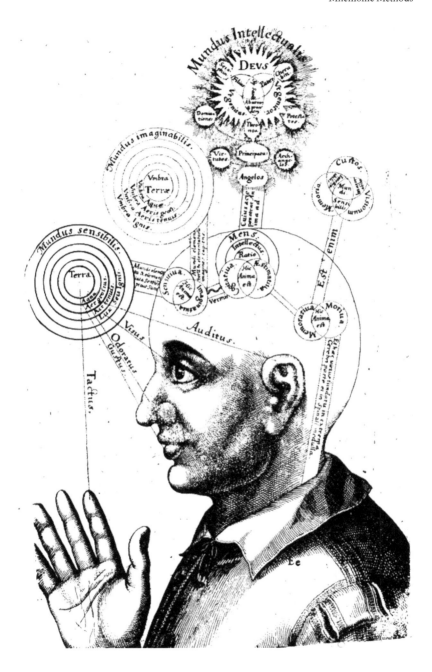

Fig. 9. The ventricular and sensory 'harmonies' according to Fludd's
Utriusque Cosmi, II.a.I, p. 217. Note the 'vermis'.

Legends for fig. 9 – see illustration opposite.

					Mundus Intellectualis: Intellectual World **DEUS**: GOD **Pater**: Father **Filius**: Son **Spiritus Sanctus**: Holy Ghost **Ab utroque procedent**: From each proceed... **Ut genitas**: As begotten **Ut genitor**: As begetter **Seraphim**: Seraphim **Cherubim**: Cherubim **Dominationes**: Dominions or Lordships **Potestates**: Powers or Authorities **Thronos**: Thrones **Virtutes**: Virtues or Strongholds **Principatus**: Principalities or Rulers **Archangelos**: Archangels **Angelos**: Angels	
	Mundus imaginabilis: Imaginable world **Umbra Terrae**: The Shadow of Earth **Umbra Aquae**: The Shadow of Water **Umbra Aeris grossi**: The Shadow of Coarse Air **Umbra Aeris tenuis**: The Shadow of Fine Air **Umbra Ignis**: The Shadow of Fire				**Cuius acie penetrat anima ad**: With whose sharpness (that of the Mind, Intellect and Reason) the soul penetrates to (the celestial powers in the panel above)	**Est enim Memoria**: For Memory is... **Custos Visionum**: The Guardian of the Visions **Mundi Sensibilis**: of the Sensible World **Intelligibilis**: of the Intelligible World **Imaginabilis**: of the Imaginable World
Mundus sensibilis: The Sensible World **Terra**: Earth **Aqua**: Water **Aer grossus**: Coarse Air **Aer tenuis**: Fine Air **Lux seu ignis**: Light or Fire	**Mundi elementorum et elementatorum imagines capiens**: Capturing the images of the world of the elements and of the elemented[3]	**Hic anima est**: Here is the Soul **Sensitiva**: the Sensitive Soul **Imaginativa**: the Imaginative Soul **Mundi elementa et elementata sentiens prout sunt**: Sensing the elements and elemented of the world just as they are.	**Vermis**: The choroid plexus		**Mens**: Mind **Intellectus**: Intellect **Ratio**: Reason **Hic anima est**: Here is the Soul **Cogitativa**: the Cogitative Soul **Aestimativa**: the Judgmental Soul	^^^^^^^^^^^
Tactus: Touch **Gustus**: Taste **Odoratus**: Smell **Visus**: Vision **Auditus**: Hearing						**Hic anima est**: Here is the Soul **Memorativa**: the Memorative Soul **Motiva**: the Motive Soul
						Et haec virtus fundatur in extrema cerebri parte et in spinali medulla: And this power has its foundation in the outer part of the brain and in the spinal cord.

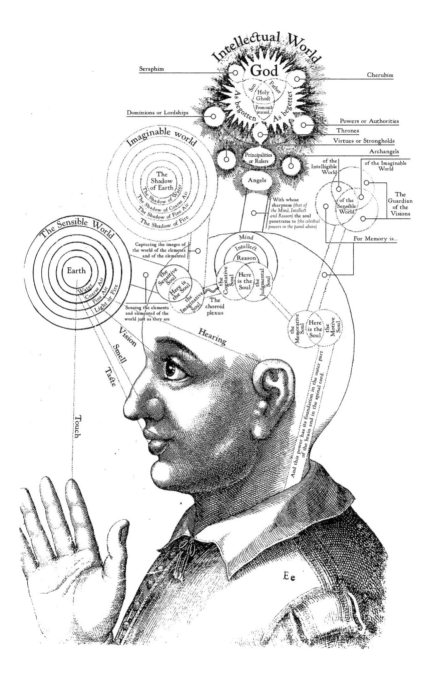

directement dans le crâne, communiquant avec l'âme; le monde sensible composé des quatre éléments, communique avec les cinq sens. Puis une sphère, dite du «monde imaginable» et correspondant aux sensations, toutes métaphysiques, de l'imagination et produites, comme celles du rêve, par des objets inexistants, par conséquent par des ombres d'éléments; c'est pourquoi nous voyons un système de sphères exactement calqué sur le précédent, et contenant l'ombre de la Terre, l'ombre de l'Eau, l'ombre de l'Air épais, l'ombre de l'Air subtil et enfin l'ombre du Feu. La sphère intellectuelle et la sphère imaginative sont reliées bizarrement par un «ver» sinueux et ténu. Enfin, l'auteur place en arrière du crâne la sphère «mémorative, ou du souvenir», qu'il fait communiquer avec la moelle épinière.

"[The diagram] shows how the upper world acts upon the human brain… It is the celestial world, composed of God and the angels, which penetrates directly into the cranium thus communicating with the soul, while the perceptible world, composed of the four elements, communicates with the five senses. Then there is a sphere called that of the 'imaginable world', corresponding to the entirely metaphysical sensations of the imagination, which are produced like those of dreams by non-existent objects and, consequently, by the shadows of elements. That is why we see a system of spheres which is an exact copy of the preceding one, and which contains the shadow of Earth, the shadow of Water, the shadow of coarse Air, the shadow of subtle Air, and, lastly, the shadow of Fire. *The intellectual sphere and the imaginative sphere are oddly linked by a slender, sinuous 'worm-like' structure.* Finally, at the back of the skull the author places the sphere which he calls the *memorative* sphere, or that of memory which, he says, communicates with the spinal marrow." (my italics)

We mentioned above that Fludd drew a major distinction between natural and artificial memory, and Chapters II and III of the First Book make it clear that the vermiform structure has an important role to play in this distinction. As Fludd says in Chapter II:

"There is, however, a difference in the way in which the two kinds of memory retain images. While the natural memory retains images of events exactly as they occurred, the artificial memory complements the natural memory with images contrived and conceived by the imagination. This is why medical people say that natural memory retains the appearances of objects through the contraction of a 'worm', or rather of a vermiform ('worm-shaped') structure located in the mid-brain, and that such appearances are forgotten again when that 'worm' stretches or extends."

And then in Chapter III, describing the so-called 'artificial memory':

"When the imagination presents fictitious images to the channel that contains the vermiform process the latter introduces them, by its extension [*dilatatio*], into that chamber of the brain where the reasoning faculty is located, where they can be carefully and rationally assessed. From there they are sent immediately to the memory-chamber so that, within the pit of that chamber, they can be captured and stored there by the self-contraction of the vermiform process."

Now there is a terminological issue here, which concerns Fludd's use of the word *dilatatio*. In Later Latin this word usually means *extension*, in other words a a vertical movement, but it can sometimes mean *dilation*, in other words a horizontal movement. To confuse matters still further, in mediaeval religious writings, such as those of Richard of St. Victor – which are not dissimilar to Neoplatonism in character – the term can be used to describe a higher mystical state in which the soul expands and is torn away from the body, e.g.:

[In his De contemplatione] "Richard abandons the attempt to reach God by reasoning powers and substitutes feeling for reflection. He distinguishes six stages in the mystical ascension of the soul towards God. In the higher stages the soul is expanded, raised above itself, delivered from itself (*dilatatio, sublevatio, alienatio, excessus*). However, whether you call him a mystic or a rationalist, Richard teaches a kind of Neo-Platonic emanation and the identity of nature and of grace." (Alfred Weber, *History of Philosophy*, p. 231).

Whether that meaning is relevant here I am not sure, but it would certainly not be inappropriate. If we take *dilatatio* to signify a vertical rather than a horizontal movement then, physiologically speaking, natural and artificial memory are quite different. But the point is moot.

Although fig. 9 does not appear in the memory-treatise, we must assume that its original readers would have studied the earlier section in which it did appear, and it should therefore be seen as an indispensable guide to the esoteric aspects of Fludd's memory-system. We have therefore translated the legends to enable the student to examine the diagram with keener understanding. Martin Faulks has also suggested that it could itself be used as a memory-palace, a theme to which we shall return below.

We now have a reasonably clear picture of the structure of brain organisation that Fludd would have inherited from his predecessors, and how he embellished it with his own Rosicrucian and Cabbalistic ideas. Now we need to investigate how this paradigm might have been used as a magical system.

V – From Memory to Magic I: All the World's a Stage, or a Temple?

As Frances Yates says in her Preface to *The Art of Memory*, "The manipulation of images in memory must always to some extent involve the *psyche* as a whole." This is axiomatic, but it took the Western world some considerable time to shift from a purely mundane to an esoteric view of the memory-arts.

Fludd uses a theatre (Chapter X of the First Book) as his memory-palace, and it is likely that this idea was not original to him but was borrowed from an earlier Italian writer who, appropriately enough, brought about the 'paradigm shift' from an exoteric to an esoteric treatment of mnemonics. Giulio Camillo (born around 1480) forms the subject of Chapters VI and VII of Yates' *Art of Memory*. It is well known that Camillo never wrote (or, at least, never published) the great treatise on the art of memory that we are sure he intended to write, but the posthumous *L'idea del theatro dell'eccellen. M. Giulio Camillo* published in Venice in 1550 is sufficiently detailed to have enabled Frances Yates and her sister to reconstruct Camillo's theatre in some detail, together with its Hermetic and Cabbalistic features.

Camillo seems to have built a large wooden scale-model of his memory theatre, explaining to those he showed around it that, within it "everything the human mind can conceive of but which we cannot see with our physical eyes can be gathered together by careful meditation and then expressed by certain physical images in such a way that we may see in them with those physical eyes everything that is otherwise concealed in the depths of the human mind" (Letter to Erasmus from Wigle Aytta van Zwichem (Viglius) in Erasmus, *Epistolae*). This points to a meditational system, not a magical one, but the famous anecdote told by Giuseppe Betussi in his dialogue *Il Raverta* suggests that Camillo may have used his theatre as a magical instrument. According to Betussi's account, Camillo was wandering around a zoo with some VIPs when a lion escaped from his cage and bounded towards them. Camillo alone stood his ground while the lion padded up to him and nuzzled against him like a pet cat before being quietly led back to his cage. For the astonished onlookers Camillo was clearly a Magus who had acquired (through his theatre?) the 'virtue' of the Sun, the ruling orb of all lions. As Yates also recounts, the Renaissance Latin poet Toscanus, in his *Peplus Italiae*, was in no doubt about the source of Camillo's powers: "Signor Camillo is very learned in the Cabbala", he says in a note, "and in the philosophies of the Egyptians (i.e. Hermeticism), Pythagoreans and Platonists". The translations of Marsilio Ficino had enabled Camillo to access this vital body of work.

Whatever the finer points of Camillo's system, we must assume that Fludd was aware of it and was influenced by it. What Camillo represents, as Yates makes clear, is a step-change from a Scholastic towards a Christian Hermeticist view of the memory-art. One thing is certain: once that change had been made, there was no going back.

We have just heard how Camillo actually built a memory-theatre or, at least, a scale-model of one. Now, Fludd devotes an entire chapter (Chapter VI of the First Book) to attacking those memory-artists who use purely imaginary memory-palaces rather than ones they have actually lived in, or, at least, have seen with their own eyes. He is quite insistent on this point – in fact the chapter reads as a rather pernickety telling-off of less competent memory-artists. Could this be a coded message to the reader that the memory-palace has to be *built* not just in the artist's imagination,but in *reality*, as a temple where the theurgist could use Fludd's techniques to develop powers beyond those of the ordinary human being?

There are two contemporary sources for Fludd's theatre-concept which may be worth mentioning. In 1618, in other words during the publication-period of the *Utriusque Cosmi*, John Willis published his

Mnemonica, sive Reminiscendi Ars in Latin, with an English translation following three years later. Willis also used stage-type structures as his memory-palaces, and the other parallels between his system and that of Fludd are too striking to be purely coincidental, including a single theatre divided by a pillar in Willis's system (corresponding to Fludd's two theatres), the use of different colours, and even a 'Day/Night' contrast for remembering different types of object. Willis, who is probably best known today for his shorthand system (*The Art of Stenographie*, 1602), was rector of Bentley Parva in Essex at the time he published his work on memory, and does not seem to have been an esotericist, so the similarities may be purely coincidental. Another, much more exciting, parallel is described by Frances Yates in Chapter XVI of her *Art of Memory*, where she speculates that Fludd's theatre may reproduce some of the features of the newly-rebuilt Globe playhouse made famous by Shakespeare.

Might these two contemporary echoes have also had an esoteric aspect? See Svenn-Arve Myklebost's paper *Early Modern visual-verbal esoteric imagery and the theatre: Julius Caesar 1.3*, available as a free download on the Internet for an insight into how "polysemous images and imagery are recombined within circular designs (wheels, spheres, globes, playhouses) upon which 'actors' are 'staged', in order to facilitate spiritual and practical insight into the micro- and the macrocosm."

VII – From Memory to Magic II: a Method?

Now the time has come to try to knit together all these insights to form a plausible explanation of how Fludd's memory-system might have been put to esoteric use.

To recap:

1. In Fludd's system, artificial memory is 'superior' to natural memory, and the Round Art is more sophisticated than the Square Art. Therefore it is reasonable to suppose that artificial memory would have been joined to the Round Art to form the basis of Fludd's system.

2. The Round Art is astrological in character and includes decanic imagery similar in outline to Bruno's system.

3. Fludd was steeped in both the Cabbala and Neoplatonism, albeit

probably only through Ficino's translations. He favoured the theurgist Iamblichus over other Neoplatonists.

4. Fludd's medical training and anatomical knowledge seem to have led him to adopt the ventricular theory. He would have thought of memory in neurological terms.

5. Fludd was influenced by Rosicrucianism, though he was not necessarily a member of the Brotherhood.

6. He was probably not directly influenced by Bruno but worked along independent lines.

7. It is probably impossible to fully comprehend his memory system without an understanding of the earlier parts of the *Utriusque Cosmi*.

8. Like Camillo, Fludd saw his memory-theatre as a real building, not merely a work of the imagination.

In the light of these suppositions, and assuming that my theory about Fludd's ideal theatre being real rather than imaginary is correct, then we can imagine the Magus working within his or her 'temple' with appropriate visual effects (decanic imagery). The time of the ritual would be determined astrologically and the Theatre decorated accordingly. The Artist would seek to forcefully internalise – as it were, 'swallow' – an image or series of images of deities or whatever using the artificial memory technique mentioned above, whereby (depending on how we interpret the term *dilatatio*) the vermiform process first *expands* to introduce the magical images to the Reason before they are 'captured' by the *contraction* of the vermis. This might involve the 'looking upwards' technique to raise the choroid plexus as suggested by Qusta ibn Luqa which we mentioned earlier. Whereas in Neoplatonic theurgy the image is magically 'charged' or animated before the Artist attempts to internalise it, in Fludd's system the 'charging' or animation is performed inside his or her mind in accordance with fig. 9. The qualities of the respective deity can then, by an effort of the imagination, be integrated into the Artist for his or her own personal use or for onward transfer to others, e.g. a 'healing' deity might be used to treat an illness the Magus is suffering from or to develop his or her own healing powers. This process stimulates the production of the *ros-a* or heavenly dew which we encountered in the quotations from Manly Palmer Hall above.

For the sake of example I shall focus on one possible magical use of Fludd's memory-system, namely *statue animation*, which was popular with some Neoplatonists. I have chosen it because Fludd himself admitted to having had some experience of it or, at least, of something very similar: as I have already said above, Fludd had admitted in his *Apologia Compendiaria* that he had "by diligence in this art, prepared a wooden ox, which, like a natural ox, alternately moves and roars; a dragon, moving its wings and hissing, which spits out of its jaws fire and flames against the ox; a lyre, which, of its own motive, plays a symphony and many other things, about which I must confess that they cannot be done by mere mathematics without the co-operation of natural magic".

For this section I am indebted to Todd Krulak's paper *Powers and Poieseis, Statue Animation and Divine Manifestation in Proclus Diadochus' Commentary on the Timaeus*, in: *Divine Powers in Late Antiquity* (Oxford, 2017), and all quotations are from this.

As Krulak says, "the Greek Magical Papyri assume that divine potency could be ritually harnessed for the accomplishment of an array of tasks including epiphany, prophecy and healing… one ingredient in this mixture was theurgy… a ritual programme designed to purify the soul and facilitate its liberation from the encosmic region and the material world… with the ultimate aim of unification with the One".

In statue animation "a divine image was ritually prepared for illumination by a deity, which resulted in both a mantic and cathartic experience for the ritual expert". It is important to understand that, in the animation ritual, it is the Magus who is the actor and not the gods, angels, daemons or whatever the Magus is interacting with. This is consistent with Fludd's distinction between the 'passive' natural memory and the active and dynamic artificial memory.

One important issue is the deity's length of stay in the image: "For the Platonists, the visitation was not expected to be one of great length, whereas the specific intent of the ritual in the *Asclepius* was to ensure that the deity had a 'long stay amongst humankind' (Asclepius 38.)."

Now one way of ensuring a 'long stay amongst humankind' is obviously to internalise the deity's image through the art of memory and then store it in the 'spice-box' (to use Fludd's idiosyncratic term), where it presumably both takes on a life of its own and is also ready for retrieval at any future moment.

The Neoplatonist Proclus also emphasises the importance of the *clarity* and *purity* – we might say, the 'sharpness' – of the image to be absorbed:

"[Statues] that obtain a dimmer divine presence enjoy the secondary and tertiary powers of the divine, but those which obtain a clear presence participate in the very first and highest productive acts of the divine, the god who was initiator of the cosmos made it appear most beautiful as an image of the very first of the eternal beings." (lines 330-31 of his *Commentary on the Timaeus*.)

For 'statues' we can here fairly substitute the word 'images', and argue that the sharper the memory-image that the Magus absorbs the more powerful and productive it is likely to be.

Krulak also quotes Proclus on the relationship between the deities and even quite mundane material objects:

"...one can see that the properties (ἰδιότητες) which are contained in the sun in a concentrated form (συνεσπειραμένας) are to be found in a 'divided-up state' amongst those entities who partake of the sun's qualities: angels, daemons, [human] souls, animals, plants, and stones" (Proclus, CMAG, VI, 150).

So an object such as a lyre can be seen as 'a little bit of Apollo' and can be worked into the magical memory-system accordingly. The problems associated with trying to visualise abstract entities can therefore be resolved by finding suitable physical analogues, as Fludd does in, for example, Chapter IV of his Second Book.

The Neoplatonists seem to have used physical statues as their images, and I suppose that painted or even sculpted images of the scenes and objects that Fludd mentions could be used in his system. This is not an important issue, as what matters is the process of 'transferring' the image from its source – whether three-dimensional, two-dimensional or purely imaginary – to its final destination in the *myrothecium*, the 'box of sweet ointments', as Fludd terms it, where the Magus stores all his or her chosen images. In the Square Art these will be drawn from the *Mundus sensibilis* and the *Mundus imaginabilis*, to use the terminology of fig. 9. In the Round Art the imagery will be drawn from the *Mundus Intellectualis* and passed through the filter of the Intellect before storage in the memory.

VII – Endings

I fully appreciate that this essay has raised far more questions than it has answered. Yates wrestled with Fludd's ideas on memory, while Craven was content to merely list them. Yates saw the esoteric possibilities of those ideas, whereas Craven I think did not. The latter's famous biography ends touchingly with an illustration of a window in Milgate Chantry, the 14th century chantry which belonged to the Fludds from the 1560s until 1624 and which is located to the north of the aisle in Robert Fludd's last resting-place, Holy Cross Church in Bearsted:

"In the Milgate Chantry are two windows opening out to the north. These had been filled with stained glass, which has now entirely disappeared, with the exception of two small portions which remain in the small spaces at the tops of the two light intersections. The fragment in the window nearest the chancel represents what may be either the Flood of Noah or some part of a scheme of the creation of the world.

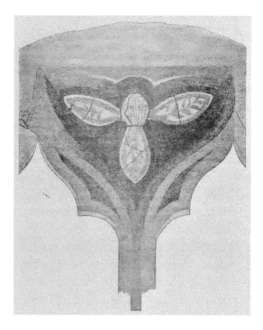

Fig. 10. The white rose window in Milgate Chantry. Here again also we have the bee symbolism which is such an important part of so many spiritual traditions, including Rosicrucianism (see fig. 8).

From clouds issue rain streams. These descend into the waters below. The space in the other window answering to this is filled with a wreathing of white roses with yellow centres." (fig.10)

I cannot look at this image without being strongly reminded of the *Filius-Pater-Spiritus Sanctus* part of the engraving in fig. 9. As Craven concludes, "These poor fragments [of stained glass] make us deeply regret that the other portions have disappeared." Like our understanding of Fludd himself they are fragmentary and enigmatic, and until we have a complete English-language edition of the *Utriusque Cosmi* we shall probably only ever be able to acquire a partial understanding of the work and ideas of the man from a humble Kent village who surely deserves to be known as the English (or Welsh!) Leonardo.

Footnotes to Introduction

1   For more about Wallace's lost ship, see Paul Ferguson, *Where is the Ship of William Wallace?* at https://www.academia.edu/37917652/WHERE_IS_THE_SHIP_OF_WILLIAM_WALLACE.

2   Readers who wish to explore Bruno's ideas more fully and compare them with Fludd's will find further information in Frances Yates's *Giordano Bruno and the Hermetic Tradition* and Chapters IX to XIII of her *Art of Memory*) as well as in the Introductions to our *Hermetic Art of Memory* (Lewis Masonic).

3   Combinations of elements (which latter are understood as minimal, dimensionless particles).

WORKS CONSULTED

Blavatsky, Helena: Collected Writings vol. XII (Theosophical Publishing House, Wheaton, 1980).

Burton, Robert: The Anatomy of Melancholy (Oxford, 1621).

Camillo, Giulio: L'idea del theatro dell'eccellen. M. Giulio Camillo (Venice, 1550).

Craven, J.B.: Doctor Robert Fludd, the English Rosicrucian (William Peace & Son, Kirkwall, 1902).

Davidson, Adele: Shakespeare in Shorthand: The Textual Mystery of King Lear (Associated University Press, 2009), p. 50f on John Willis.

Dicsone, Faulks, Ferguson: The Hermetic Art of Memory (Lewis Masonic, 2020).

Dolce, Lodovico: Dialogo di M. Lodovico Dolce, nel quale si ragiona del modo di accrescere, & conservar la Memoria (Venice, 1586).

Erasmus, Desiderius: Epistolae.

Fludd, Robert: Apologia Compendiaria Fraternitatem de Rosea Cruce Suspicionis et Infamiae Maculis Aspersam (Leiden, 1616).

Fludd, Robert: Musica Mundana, translated by Paul Ferguson as On the Music of the Spheres, with a CD of Fludd's music (MOHS, Glasgow, 2009).

Fludd, Robert: Sophiae cum Moria Certamen (Frankfurt, 1629).

Fludd, Robert (attributed): Summum Bonum, (Frankfurt, 1629).

Fludd, Robert: Utriusque Cosmi, Maioris scilicet et Minoris, metaphysica, physica, atque technica Historia (Oppenheim & Frankfurt, 1617-24).

Fuller, Dr. Thomas: History of the Worthies of England, (London, 1662).

Givry, Grillot de: Le Musée des Sorciers, Mages et Alchimistes (Librairie de France, Paris, 1929).

Godwin, Joscelyn: Robert Fludd, Hermetic Philosopher and Surveyor of Two Worlds (Thames & Hudson, 1979).

Gordon, Bernard de: Affectus praeternaturam curandi Methodus (1296).

Gordon, Bernard de: Practica dicta Lilium medicine (1305).

Green, Christopher D.: Where did the Ventricular Localization of Mental Faculties come from? (JHBS, Vol. 39(2), 131–142 Spring 2003).

Hall, Manly P.: Man, the Grand Symbol of the Mysteries, especially

Chapter X (The Philosophers Press, 1937).

Heydon, John: Theomagia, or The temple of wisdome (H. Brome & T. Rooks, 1662-64).

Jennings, Hargrave: The Rosicrucians, their Rites and Mysteries (Chatto & Windus, 1879).

Krulak, Todd: Powers and Poiēseis, in: Divine Powers in Late Antiquity (Oxford, 2017).

Montagnana, Petrus de: Fasciculus Medicine (1491).

Myklebost, Svenn-Arve: Early Modern visual-verbal esoteric imagery and the theatre: Julius Caesar 1.3

Ovason, David: Shakespeare's Secret Booke, Deciphering Magical and Rosicrucian Codes (Clairview, 2010).

Prinke, Rafał: The Great Work in the Theatre of the World, in: A Compendium on the Rosicrucian Vault, ed. Adam McLean, Edinburgh 1985.

Reisch, Gregorius: Margarita Philosophica, (Per Sebastianum Henricpetri, Basel, 1583).

Shoja, M.M et al: History of the Pineal Gland, in Childs Nerv Syst (2016) 32:583–586.

Singer, Charles: 'Scientific Views and Visions of St. Hildegard', in Studies in the History of Method of Science, vol. I (OUP, 1917).

Smith & Whitaker: Ventricular Psychology, in: Brain, Mind and Consciousness in the History of Neuroscience (Springer Science & Business, 2014).

Trevelyan, W.C. & Combe, George: 'Early Opinions about Functions of the Brain', in: Selections from the Phrenological Journal, (Edinburgh 1836).

Vesalius, Andreas: De Humani Corporis Fabrica, (Ex officina Joannis Oporini, Basel,1543).

Walker, D.P.: Spiritual and Demonic Magic from Ficino to Campanella (Warburg Institute, London, 1958).

Weber, Alfred, transl. Thilly: History of Philosophy (Scribner's Sons, New York, 1904).

Weisse, Dr. John A.: The Obelisk and Freemasonry (Bouton, New York, 1880).

Willis, John: Mnemonica, sive Reminiscendi Ars (Humphrey Lownes, 1618).

Yates, Frances: Giordano Bruno and the Hermetic Tradition (London and Chicago, 1964).

Yates, Frances: The Art of Memory, especially Chapter XV (Routledge, London, 1966).

Part I:
Treatise I, Section II, Part III, Book I
of the
Utriusque cosmi maioris scilicet et minoris

CHAPTER I
in which we learn about the author's diligent endeavours mastering and perfecting the Art of Memory in foreign lands.

During my wanderings around Europe, I made a special point of exploring the Kingdom of France, crossing that nation from West to East. I finally headed for the city of Nîmes, attracted there by the great fame of its surviving antiquities. It was in Nîmes that I first savoured the delights of the Art of Memory, through studying it with someone in that city who was quite well-known for his mnemonic skills. Soon afterwards I moved to Avignon, a city on the Rhone, where I once again worked extremely hard at mastering this Art, but this time without the aid of a teacher. When I had acquired sufficient expertise in this field, I was summoned by certain French aristocrats in various parts of Provence to act as their tutor, partly because of my expertise in the Art of Memory but also because of my knowledge of certain branches of mathematics. My pupils included the Marquis d'Oraison, the Vicomte de Cadenet, and a man whom the locals spoke of with awe as a great prince, namely the Bishop of Riez[2].

Finally, after rejecting other (even more lucrative) offers of tutorial work, I arrived in Marseilles, where I began teaching mathematics to the Duke of Guise[3], his younger brother the Prince of Lorraine[4], and to this Knight of Malta[5]. The last of these three gentlemen was a young man of outstanding character and also of fine physique to whom I taught, among other subjects, the Art of Memory. Indeed, he displayed such remarkable intelligence that, within a very short time, he had surpassed the other two noblemen in his level of understanding.

So, to summarise, I went first to Nîmes, then to Avignon, then to Aix-en-Provence, and finally to Marseilles, where I thoroughly and passionately investigated the more recondite areas[6] of this science, in which I both saw and learned things of great interest.

And now, dear reader, I shall freely share with you all those matters in which I invested such considerable expense and effort.

CHAPTER II

in which we learn what Memory is, and of how many parts it consists, as well as how to capture and retain the images that are associated with the two kinds of Memory.

Since I intend to proceed methodically, I think it is important, before I discuss the Art of Memory in more detail, to give you some idea of what memory actually is.

We can define it as *the most faithful guardian and conservator of things perceived, as well as of images or objects whose appearances have been grasped by the intellect.* Alternatively, it can be seen as *a state of mind that reproduces, after a certain length of time, the appearances of objects that are always in the past.*

Of course, human beings and the lower animals both have a memory-function, but I want the reader to understand that human memory differs from that of the lower animals in that the latter is purely sensory, receiving only sense-perceptions and the phantasms of objects, whereas human memory is simultaneously both sensory and *intellectual.*

If we carefully consider this distinction we can see that the intellectual memory needs to be considered from two points of view, namely either in its *natural* disposition (the character of which we have already explained in the above definition) or alternatively in the sense of a *skill* by which something can be recalled to mind. This latter type we call *artificial memory*, since it is assisted by the precepts of that skill that we call the Art of Memory.

We can therefore define *artificial memory* as an operation of the *natural memory which is performed by means of a skill*, and we can argue that this skill is, in its turn, based on a performance of the imagination. It will be clear from this statement that, in itself, artificial memory without natural memory is as much use as trying to understand numerals without the concept of fingers.

There is, however, a difference in the way in which the two kinds of memory retain images. While the natural memory retains images of events exactly as they occurred, the artificial memory complements the natural memory with images contrived and conceived by the imagination. This is why medical people say that natural memory retains the appearances of objects through the contraction of a 'worm', or rather of a vermiform ('worm-shaped') structure[7] located in the mid-brain, and that such appearances are forgotten again when that 'worm' stretches or extends.

An artificial memory on the other hand is usually retained by means of the constant activity of the imagination as it impresses images of objects or events into the spice-box[8] of the memory. This, at least, is what usually happens, due to the propinquity of the imagination to (and the juxtaposition of its action with) that chamber of the brain in which the memory is located. Since the relevant act of the imagination has been freshly created and is now permanent, it knocks assiduously at the door of the memory and, as if by a living action (albeit one achieved using contrived and inanimate images) projects to it by means of constant impulses the image that needs to be retained, just as a mute person tries to point out and explain something to another person by using signs rather than words.

CHAPTER III
in which we examine whether an artificial memory can be acquired or developed by any means other than by the power of the imagination.

So we are agreed that the natural memory can be strengthened in one of two ways: either by the *assiduous operation of the imaginative faculty*, which inscribes in the memory impressions of actual objects and events through representations of fictitious ones, or *through the power of medicines* to restore a natural memory that has become unreliable.

When the imagination presents fictitious images to the channel that contains the vermiform process the latter introduces them, by its extension[9], into that chamber of the brain where the reasoning faculty is located, where they can be carefully and rationally assessed. From there they are sent immediately to the memory-chamber so that, within the pit of that chamber, they can be captured and stored there by the self-contraction of the vermiform process.

Medicines are also beneficial in cases where the memory has been impaired by an unnatural injury, by excessive and sudden cold and damp or, conversely, by excessive heat and dryness. Indeed, even the imagination itself can be harmed by an unnatural excess of these, but an injured imagination can be repaired and restored to its natural state by medicines, a subject about which medical people have written extensively. However, the physicians and medical writers have not discovered any way of alleviating a weak memory other than by these two methods, i.e. imagination and medication, apart from that unique gift that is sometimes imparted to the chosen few by supernatural agency and which is inspired in them in exceptional circumstances by the divine grace and glory.

CHAPTER IV
in which we consider the imagination's twofold action with regard to the artificial memory.

There are two ways in which the imagination helps us achieve utter perfection in the Art of Memory. The first is by *ideas* which, properly speaking, are forms separated from corporeal things. These include spirits, shadows, souls and so on, as well as angels, with which we are chiefly concerned in our Round Art (see below), for in this case we are not using the word 'idea' in the Platonic sense to mean the mind of God, but rather to signify anything that is not composed of the four elements, in other words some simple thing conceived by the imagination in the ethereal or spiritual part of the world, such as angels, demons, the constellations, or the images of the gods or goddesses to whom celestial phenomena are assigned and who are by nature more spiritual than corporeal. We also include in this category the shadows of the virtues and vices as conceived and fashioned in the imagination, for these must also be regarded as demons. Should the pupil fail to find suitable images representing ideas of this kind to imprint in their mind, then they can choose whatever animals, human beings or inanimate objects they wish, and can conceive of their images standing at the cardinal points instead of shadows and ideas.

But there is another way in which the imagination can achieve utter perfection in the Art of Memory, and that is by using *images of corporeal things* which, although they are perceived by way of the imagination, are not regarded as incorporeal but rather as things derived from corporeal action and fashioned by the imagination alone, e.g. we may imagine a wolf killing a lamb, Peter swallowing a knight's broad-bladed sword sharpened to the finest of points[10], a venomous snake entwining its sinuous coils around the thigh of an acquaintance, and so on, for the Memory Artist should use only his imagination and fantasy to consider things that are perceptible to the senses, in other words he should fashion those things in his imagination in the same way as a painter does when he uses vivid colours to depict and elaborate visible objects.

From the foregoing we can conclude that the memory can only be artificially corrected by medicines or by an effort of the imagination by which it concerns itself either with ideas (which, properly speaking, are the domain of the *Round Art*) or with the images of corporeal things, which are more suited to the *Square Art.* That is why we are unable to agree with those Memory Artists who do not use either medicines or the imagination. Such people are only convinced they can do so either because they are completely untutored in Natural Philosophy or because they have been led astray by certain loud-mouthed rascals and impostors into thinking that it is perfectly natural for the Art of Memory to be learned entirely without ideas and images. I recall that a certain lawyer from Aix-en-Provence was of this stamp, boldly asserting that he knew someone in Toulouse who claimed to have developed a perfect memory by using the Ring and Wand of Solomon[11] which, indeed, if it has ever been done, we strenuously deny could ever have been accomplished by natural means, even though we concede that such a thing could perhaps truly and infallibly occur through the deceitful powers of demons or by the metaphysical influence of the Holy Spirit. However, in order to ensure the complete perfection of a natural phenomenon, the *imagination* must assist in a metaphysical act, for the imagination is a sort of entrance or doorway to the memory, through which every kind of perceptible phenomenon to be preserved in the memory-chamber must enter.

Fig. 2. *The Wand of Solomon, from the* Clavicula Salamonis[12].

CHAPTER V
in which we consider whether the Art of Memory is more conveniently expressed through the Round Art or the Square Art.

Our *Spherical or Round* Art is undoubtedly much easier to use, partly due to the nature of the image employed which, being round, is more suited to the task; partly because any place upon the sphere finds its natural distribution in any sphere of the terrestrial globe; and partly because every sphere has its natural site and position without any change of that position, which means that the operator can be certain that he is always looking at the same unchanging *loci*[13], and that no planet will move or deviate outside its orbit but, to use an astrological term, will always 'joy' in its own proper sphere with its own operation, action and dominion. Our Spherical Art therefore assists most wonderfully with the natural memory of the Microcosm and, by virtue of the relationship it enjoys with parts and activities of that Microcosm, has a great deal to offer in many other respects

In the *Square Art* on the other hand nothing is natural – neither *locus*, distributions nor images – and yet those inexperienced in Astronomy tend to prefer square *commonplaces*[14] as they are called in the Art, since square halls, rooms, closets or whatever are more readily imprinted in the minds of unlettered people than ideas arrived at through contemplation alone. As a result, most people prefer the Square Art to the Round Art, even though the latter is much more useful than the former and is also more natural, although admittedly the Square Art is more akin to an art and is also more susceptible to sense-impressions.

CHAPTER VI
in which we discuss the great error of some Memory Artists, and in particular refute the arguments of those who use purely imaginary memory-palaces.

Some Memory Artists have tried to locate their Square Art in memory-palaces that they have newly designed or 'built' using the power of their imaginations. We shall now briefly explain how inappropriate this approach is.

If we compare the functions of the imagination or fantasy with those of what we know about the human eye we can see that the latter behaves quite differently. If, for example, we line up a series of mirrors facing one another in such a way that the image of an object seen in the first mirror is reflected by that mirror in the second, and the image seen in the second mirror is again reflected in the third, and the image of the third subsequently in the fourth, and so on in all the others, then we shall certainly note that the image in the first mirror is clearer, sharper and more complete than the image in the second, and that the image in the second is clearer and so on than that in the third, and so also with the fourth and fifth. The final reflection will therefore be very obscure and, indeed, scarcely perceptible. This happens, of course, because the rays gradually weaken as they are broken down in the multiplication of reflections, so that the first reflection is stronger than the second, the second stronger than the third, and so on with all the others.

We can argue by analogy that the more the Memory Artist penetrates the more recondite recesses of his imagination, the weaker the likenesses of the exact images that take flight from his imagination will be, and therefore the more debilitated and deficient the operative power of that imagination.

It follows from this that the closer and the more immediate the relationship of the similitude produced by the imagination is to the reality of the sense-datum, the more certain, strong, durable and effective it will be when we come to use it in the Art of Memory.

Memory Artists of the kind we have described above have, however, tried to locate the basis of their activity not in reality but in a sort of chimera or figment of an object that has never actually existed in Nature, as if – using the operation of the optical function mentioned above as our analogy – we were to believe that an image not seen in the first mirror, and derived from neither truth nor reality, could still be observed in the second or third mirror, which is obviously absurd and impossible.

It is therefore inappropriate to imagine 'new' memory-palaces that have never existed anywhere at any time, for such an artificial creation will simply distract the Memory Artist from the contemplation of the truth. Instead, the memory-palace should be a *real* house, castle or palace so that, by using a commonplace that is already familiar to your senses, you may, as it were, build your house on secure foundations and in a more regular fashion, for if indeed the foundations collapse or are swept away then the whole body of it will perish and suddenly disappear which, of course, can very easily happen if the initial commonplace is a fictitious one. With an object that presents itself to the senses on the other hand there is no fear of such an accident or, at least, if something of that kind does occur, the *locus* when seen again will readily return to the memory.

What is more, as we said above when discussing the reflections in the mirrors, the further from the original the image has reached in the process of multiplication of perceptions, the weaker its impression in the memory will be. The 'fixing' of the impression will last longest if we first imagine the palace; then imagine the rooms in this or that colour, or round in shape, and so on; and then divide any one side of them into five parts and fill any of the distributions with invented images, before finally imprinting upon them by some action the things that we need to memorise.

If, however, the palace was to fall into oblivion then everything else as well – namely the rooms and their *loci* and the images and all the things that need to be remembered – would all be completely removed. Also, that action whose intensity determines whether things are retained in the memory (and which is consequently of the first importance in this Art) would be extremely weak: not only would its foundation be fictitious, but in terms of its 'fixing' in the memory it would have receded from the foundation of truth by a whole degree.

One final way in which we can show that this approach does not have any rational basis is through the following medical experiment. Even if a sufficiently strong medicine is orally administered to those suffering from a gallstone, it gradually loses some of its effectiveness in transit by leaving a part behind in the abdomen, the liver, the blood and the kidneys, so that when it finally permeates the bladder it is so weak that it is largely or entirely unable to fulfil the purpose for which it was originally infused into the body.

So, by analogy, by multiplying one imaginative invention on top of another the action of the imagination becomes progressively weaker, from which we can conclude *that the operation of the imagination starts with and proceeds from* real *things, and not from* intentional *things*, since the actions that proceed from real things and which are concealed within them are stronger, more definite and closer to the truth.

CHAPTER VII
in which we criticise those Memory Artists who, in both versions of the Art , insist that only animals should be assigned to the commonplaces.

We cannot consider people to be experts in this Art if they imprint dumb or irrational animals into the *loci* of their palace, house or rooms, even if they usually do so in alphabetical order, e.g. by allocating an *Ass* to the first position, a *Bullock* to the second, and so on. Because these animals are dumb, they simply cannot be used to stand for a rational object or an action that is a characteristic of human beings alone. The irrationality of such an image perhaps helps explain why such Memory Artists sometimes forget a rational subject, due to the sheer impossibility of the action attributed to the dumb animal in question, e.g. if we want to imprint an *orator* in the first *locus* (which in their system is an *Ass*) then we have to imagine the ass dressed as an orator with a book in his hand and a felt cap on his head, which would of course appear utterly absurd to the reasoning faculty by which human beings are governed, since asses do not have clothes, books or hands.

For this reason we think it is better and more correct to assign <u>rational</u> images to these *loci*, since there is no action, either animalistic or human, that a human being cannot eloquently express by their own actions, either by imitation or by their own characteristic behaviour. If therefore we want to express the idea of an Ass we can imagine the image of a man in the allocated *locus* jumping onto the back of an ass, or teaching an ass to read, and so on.

CHAPTER VIII
in which we criticise those who use empty spaces as loci *for memorising imaginable objects.*

Some Memory Artists commit an even graver error than the one we discussed in the previous chapter. Indeed, they seem in the process to be actually *violating the laws of Nature*, as they follow an even rockier path, and use an even worse method than the one we have already mentioned, the errors of which they considerably surpass because they use empty *loci* in which, of course, they manage to imprint nothing at all. They allocate those things that need to be remembered to those bare and naked places by frequently inculcating that well-known philosophical maxim, *frustra fit per plura, quod fieri potest per pauciora*[15], "it is pointless to do with more what can be done with fewer".

To use an analogy, we could argue that the invention of four-, five- and six-stringed musical instruments was silly and superfluous, as the entire scope of music can be accommodated within single-stringed ones, but the fact remains that expert musicians more readily produce interesting music on multi-stringed instruments than they do on ones with just a single string. Similarly, although we cannot deny that the Art of Memory is quite effective if empty *loci* are used, we would say that this is far from being a perfect or easy way of practising it, as well as making it more difficult for the student. In addition, we can definitely state that there is no distinction between the *loci* unless some figure or image, made distinctive by its fantastic appearance, is imprinted in any one of them. The error of such Memory Artists can therefore only lead to further mistakes and to not inconsiderable confusion. For that reason, if we wish to avoid befuddlement and absurdity in this Art, we need to assign distinctive images to each *locus*, as the presence of such images is the best way of distinguishing one *locus* from another.

CHAPTER IX
in which we discuss the use of commonplaces in the Round Art, and their assignment to their own loci *for the memorising of words.*

The *loci* or commonplaces used in the Round Art are always ethereal parts of the world, i.e. the celestial orbs, numbered from the eighth sphere to the lunar sphere. However, the commonplaces are distributed *in duplicate*, with each one assigned according to *locus* and *order*. This means that, in the former, we assign them in accordance with Nature to one of twelve equal parts according to that division of the Zodiac which the Astrologers have called the *celestial sign*s, and in the latter according to *time*. The latter technique involves a further subdivision, for since the first commonplace is mobile and completes its rapid course in one natural day from East to West, then any given hour of the day will correspond to fifteen[16] degrees of the Zodiac, an interval corresponding to half a sign. However, the length of a sign outlines the motion of the Sun to the extent of one hour of the day. After passing completely through the Zodiac or eighth sphere, the Sun must start in the Heaven of Saturn and then continue through the others by descending from the periphery of the mid-heaven towards the sphere of fire, as shown in the following figure.

The *temporal loci* are also duplicated. One is located in the East and faces the Eastern part of the world in that same sign: we can imagine this *locus* as being filled with a White Theatre. The other is Western or a part of the Western sign, and in it we place a Black Theatre, as we shall describe below.

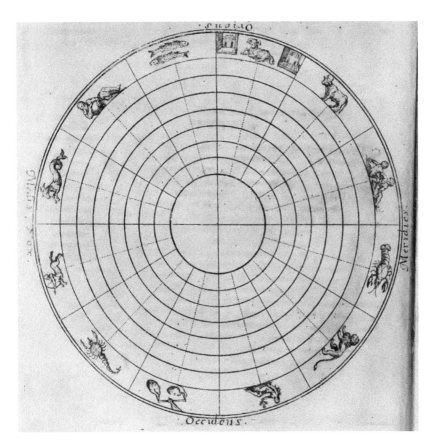

Fig. 3. *Oriens*: East/Sunrise, *Media Nox*: Midnight, *Meridies*: Noon,
Occidens: West/Sunset.

CHAPTER X
in which we describe the Eastern and Western Theatres.

By a *theatre* we mean a structure in which all the actions of words,
sentences, parts of speech or subjects can be displayed, just as they might
be in a public playhouse where comedies and tragedies are performed.

You can imagine one theatre of this kind as being located in the East.
This theatre should be seen as real or corporeal but, as it were, made of
ethereal vapour. Now fill that shadowy theatre with the likenesses of
active spirits.

The *first* theatre will be white, and will be bright and resplendent, since it represents the day and daytime actions. That is why it is placed in the East, because the Sun starts the day by rising from the East with a promise of bringing light to the world.

The *second* theatre should be imagined as painted black, and should be dark and gloomy. You can imagine it as being located in the West, for when the Sun is in that part of the sky it heralds the imminent arrival of the night and darkness.

Each of these theatres will have *five doors*, all distinct from one other, and roughly the same distance apart. We shall explain the use of these doors later.

Fig. 4. *Theatrum orbi: the theatre of the world*[17], *with the seats of the circular, square and hexagonal columns outlined on the floor.*

CHAPTER XI
in which we discuss the use of commonplaces in the Square Art and their distribution in suitable loci, *as well as the choice and arrangement of rooms for the purposes of this Art.*

In this branch of the Art a *locus* or commonplace will be a closet or room, with square or parallel sides of equal length. A room of this kind should not be fictitious or purely imaginary, as used by those who conceive a palace entirely in the mind, as this would cause confusion and obscurity in the imaginative operations and overwhelm its active force. For that reason I think you should choose *real* rooms, and more specifically ones that are distinguished by their ornateness, their beautiful outlook, or some other feature pleasing to the eye, and which are also as different from one another as possible.

Above the door of each room there should be depicted some exciting story, such as for example Hercules slaying the Hydra or prostrating Cerberus, or Medea killing her brother, or Actæon being transformed into a stag[18], and so on. All the images of stories of this kind are to be depicted externally above the doors to the rooms. To make the method more comprehensible, we show in the following table the orderings and distribution of the internal *loci* (which we call *minor commonplaces*) and the subdivisions of their parts.

	Either _External_, in which the images are displayed externally to more clearly distinguish one room from another, as if one were assigning to the rooms their own specific names.			
Locus is twofold, namely:		_Commonplaces_, six in number:	*Four square sides of a room.* *Floor or ground.* *Roof or ceiling of the room*	
	Or _Internal_, which is subdivided into *loci*, which are:			
			Less characteristic, e.g. *two exterior parallelograms, namely 1 & 3.*	
		Minor commonplaces, which are either:		
			or _More characteristic_, e.g.	*Four square parts of exterior parallels subdivided into 1. 2. 3. 4.* *Parallelogram in the middle*

We usually start with the right-hand side of the doorway, as Memory Artists should always follow the daily motion of the Sun, which starts its progress from the right-hand part of the sky and then proceeds to the left, i.e. from East to West. Those who start on the left-hand side, arguing that this is the direction in which we write, are therefore proceeding neither effectively nor methodically, for in any art it is always appropriate to imitate Nature in all one's actions.

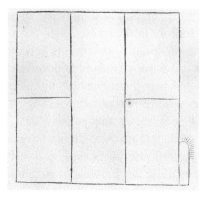

Fig. 5. *The figure of the square.*

After making the necessary divisions and subdivisions, and dividing the two outer parallelograms into two equal parts, the first of the floors of the parallelogram will serve as the *locus* of the first room, while the part projecting beyond it will be the second. The top of the second parallelogram will be the third *locus*, while its floor will be the fourth. The whole of the third parallelogram located in the middle will be the fifth and final *locus* of the same side.

We therefore have 6 square sides which, multiplied by 5, give us the 30 *loci* we need for this Art. You should proceed in the same way on all the other sides by dividing and subdividing, just as you did with the first one.

CHAPTER XII

in which we explain which image should be assigned to each of these
loci.

For the sake of greater consistency we shall assign to each of the *loci* mentioned above the image of a theatre with three doors, in the middle of which an image will be fixed which we shall call the *essential image*. Sometimes, in exceptional circumstances, we shall move the essential image from its own *locus* to another *locus* on the exterior, as will be explained later.

Fig. 6. *What the Theatre looks like.*

Part II:
Treatise I, Section II, Part III, Book II
of the
Utriusque cosmi maioris scilicet et minoris

CHAPTER I

in which we learn about certain alphabets required for memorising words, sentences, speeches and entire subjects, with particular reference to the Round Art.

Both the *Round* and *Square* Arts require *five alphabetical sequences*, the first consisting of *men*, the second of *women*, the third of *animals other than birds or fishes*, the fourth of *birds* and the fifth of *fishes*[19].

The 'men' used in the Spherical Art must either be gods or the spiritual bodies of men who have been dedicated to the stars, and they must be imagined as being without physical bodies. The same rule applies to the women, who must also be of a celestial nature.

The names of the gods and those who live with them are as follows: *Apollo* with his solar rays, *Bacchus* with his grapes, *Cupid* with his bow and quiver, *Demogorgon* (also known as *Pluto*) the god of the underworld, *Eolus*, *Faunus*, *Ganymede*, *Hymenæus*, *Jupiter*, *Lucifer*, *Mars*, *Neptune*, *Orion*, *Pan*, *Quirinus*, *Romulus*, *Saturn*, *Titan* and *Vulcan*.

The names of the goddesses and celestial women are *Andromache*, *Bellona*, *Ceres*, *Diana*, *Europa*, *Flora*, *Gorgon*, *Hyades*, *Juno*, *Lucina*, *Minerva*, *Natura*, *Opis*, *Proserpina*, *Quinquatria*, *Rumia*, *Thetis* and *Venus*.

The names of the animals are *Aries* (ram), *Bos* (ox), *Caprinus* (goat), *Delphin* (dolphin), *Equus* (horse*)*, *Felis* (cat), *Gorgoneus serpens* (the Gorgon's snake), *Hydra* (Hydra), *Iricinus*[20] (tick), *Leo* (lion), *Mulus* (mule), *Nereus*[21] (merman), *Onager* (wild ass), *Pegasus volans* (Pegasus the winged-horse), *Questor*[22], *Rhinoceros* (rhinoceros), *Scorpius* (scorpion), *Taurus* (bull) and *Ursa* (bear).

When we come to *birds*, we find there are only three in the eighth sphere, namely *Aquila* (eagle), *Vultur* (vulture) & *Corvus* (raven), so we need to complete the sequence by using spirits endowed with some kind of vice or virtue. So, for example, we can imagine *Ambitio* (ambition) gazing upwards with wings outstretched, *Bestialitas* (animality) looking downwards and covered in hair, *Crudelitas* (cruelty) holding a blood-stained sword in one hand and a pierced heart in the other, *Desperatio* (desperation) as someone hanging himself, *Ebrietas* (drunkenness) as someone holding a ladle full of wine, *Fortitudo* (strength) as someone leaning against or embracing a pillar, *Gula* (gluttony) as someone with a huge stomach who cannot stop eating, *Humilitas* (humility) as a person on bended knee, *Infamia* (infamy) as a squalid-looking person covered in grime, *Lætitia* (joy) as someone wreathed in flowers who has a happy or smiling face and is singing or dancing, *Miseria* (misery) as someone covered in rags and wasting away with illness, *Nemesis* (retribution) as bloodstained hands, *Obedientia* (obedience) as someone threatened with humiliation (see *Humilitas*), *Pudicitia* (chastity) as someone in white garments, *Querela* (lamentation) as someone roused by the flames of ire, *Religio* (religion) as someone holding a crucifix, *Spes* (hope) as a person holding a blue anchor[23], *Timor* (fear) as someone running while constantly looking behind them, *Verecundia* (moderation) as someone wearing a golden crown, and *Zelotypia* (jealousy) as a person spying on other people's activities.

The sequences of inanimate objects and their corresponding numbers are expressed either by exact representations of those objects or by simulacra of them, as we shall make clear in the two sequences that follow.

However, all these images must be imagined as *shadowy and transparent* or with *diaphanous* bodies, just as they might appear in the ethereal sphere.

CHAPTER II
in which we discuss the alphabets and names used in the Square Art.

In the Square Art the images must be conceived as acting just as they would in elemental nature, i.e. made to a certain extent of flesh and blood, but also displaying a certain refinement and subtlety.

In the case of *men*, the alphabet can be constructed from people who are well-known to you, but you are also free to choose famous historical figures. It is much better however if you choose people who are your friends or, at least, who are known to you, e.g. people called *Abraham, Bernhardus, Carolus, Daniel, Emanuel, Franciscus, Guilielmus, Henricus, Johannes, Laurentius, Matthæus, Nicolaus, Oliverius, Petrus, Quintilianus, Richardus, Salomon, Thomas, Vincentius*[24].

If you are choosing people from ancient history, then good examples would be *Achilles, Brutus, Cadmus, Diogenes, Eteocles, Fabius, Ganymed, Hercules, Jason, Leander, Midas, Nestor, Orion, Prometheus, Quintilianus, Romulus, Sinon, Tantalus, Ulysses* with Circe, *Xerxes* with his army, or *Yxion*[25] being tortured on the wheel.

Female names that might be familiar to you include *Agrippina*, *Barbara, Catharina, Dalia, Elisabetha, Francisca, Guliana, Hester, Jana, Laurina, Martha, Nerea, Oriana, Paulina, Quirina, Rosamunda, Sara, Tomisena, Valeriana*, but there are also the names of women famous in ancient history, such as *Ariadne, Bersabe, Clytemnestra, Dido, Europa, Flora, Galilæa, Helena, Jana, Lais, Medea, Niobe, Olympias (mother of Alexander the Great), Penelope, Quintiliana, Roxana, Semiranis, Tomyris* and *Vesta.*

Names of animals include *Asinus* (ass), *Bos* (ox), *Camelus* (camel), *Dama* (red deer), *Elephas* (elephant), *Felis* (cat), *Gryphus* (griffin), *Hydra* (hydra), *Jumentum* (beast of burden), *Leo* (lion), *Mulus* (mule), *Nereus serpens magnus* (great sea serpent), *Ovis* (sheep), *Panthera* (panther), *Questor* (an animal that barks like a dog[26]), *Rhinoceros* (rhinoceros, which has a horn on its forehead), *Simia* (monkey), *Tigris* (tiger) and *Ursa* (bear).

Names of birds which have been used in this Art include *Aquila* (eagle), *Bubo* (horned owl), *Corvus* (raven), *Drepanus* (martin), *Erithacus* ('the bird that lives alone'[27]), *Falco* (falcon), *Grus* (crane), *Hirundo* (swallow), *Ibis* (ibis), *Luscinia* (nightingale), *Milvus* (kite), *Noctua* (night-owl), *Olor* (swan), *Pica* (magpie), *Querquedula* (teal), *Regulus* (goldcrest), *Sturnus* (starling), *Turdus* (thrush), and *Vespertilio* (bat[28]).

And so on in the other cases. So, for example, a man sitting on the back of a donkey and holding a lance will represent the number 10, but if he is holding a fork it will mean 20, while a three-legged stool will signify 30, a book 40, and so on.

If you want to use your imagination to assign the number 11 to a certain *locus*, then you should think of two men carrying two lances. You can even express longer numbers, for example 432 by imagining on the left a man holding a book, on the right a miller or farmer with a pitchfork, and in the middle a woman sitting on a three-legged stool after she has assigned appropriate activities to each of these two individuals.

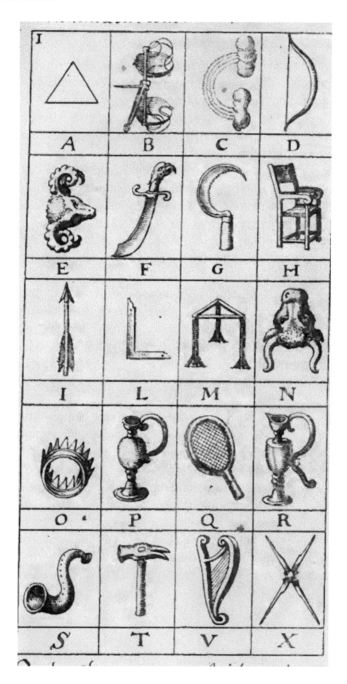

Fig. 7. *Alphabetical sequence of inanimate objects.*

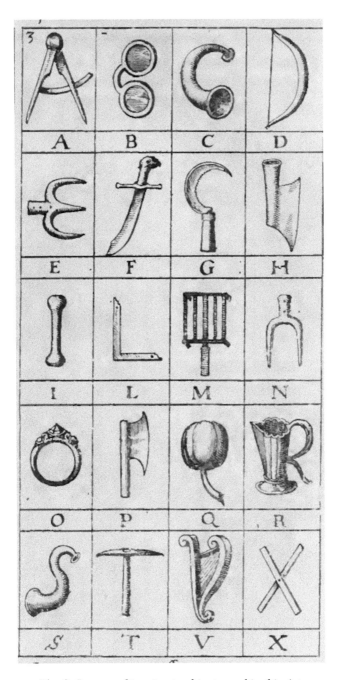

Fig. 8. *Images of inanimate objects used in this Art.*

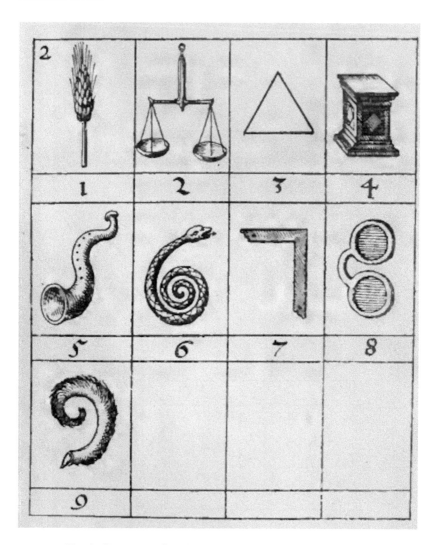

Fig. 9. *Sequence of arithmetical characters used in this Art.*

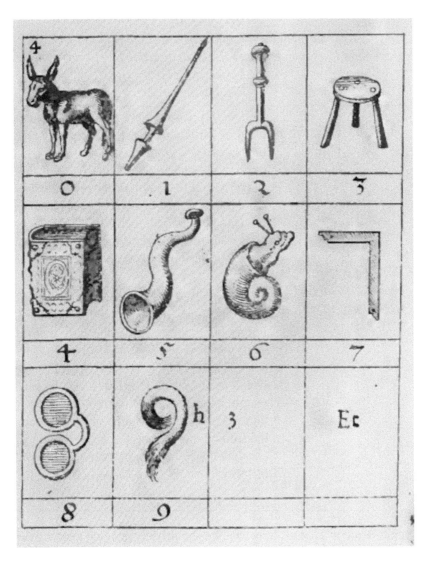

Fig. 10. *Arithmetical characters used in this Art.*[29]

CHAPTER III
in which we learn how many different conceptions of this Art there are, and to what actions they must be assigned in any locus *upon the sphere.*

The *idea* or *imaginative form* of this Art can be either:	*Principal*, i.e. it is active in every principal word or particle of a section of any speech or sentence, e.g. the image of the Ram (Aries) will appear in the first *locus* of the first circle. If the action of the predominant word is insufficient to express the object that needs to be signified, then it can be assisted by actions of the Lord of this Sign, namely Mars, but this is rarely necessary.
	Or *secondary*, which is when, in order to achieve a more striking distinction, the story is imprinted in the Eastern theatre of the sign, which is the sign of Nature. So, for example, *Jason* holding the Golden Fleece would be allocated to the first *locus*, *Medea* to the second, the shepherd *Paris* to the third, *Daphne* to the fourth, and *Phœbus* to the fifth to signify that it is a male daytime constellation, and so on in the other *Eastern theatres*.

In the *Western theatres*, however, we should only imagine the *shadows* of the forms that appear in the first theatre, and this in a dark and gloomy manner, for the colour of this theatre, since it represents the beginning of the night, usually appears dark to the eyes of the imagination.

CHAPTER IV
in which we discuss the principal sequences of ideas throughout the planetary spheres.

Throughout the sphere of Saturn the principal sequence will be as follows: the first ascending *locus* of this sphere will be *Capricorn*, and so on according to the succession of the Signs, for Capricorn is the daytime house of Saturn. So *Saturn* in ♑ *is a king of great wealth,* in ♒ *an experienced general of sound judgement,* in ♓ *a fisherman,* in ♈ *angry and jealous,* in ♉ *inconstant and self-indulgent,* in ♊ *a babbler, yet very learned and prudent,* in ♋ *a merchant saddened by financial loss,* in ♌ *a prosperous and dignified old man,* in ♍ *a wise man, but one who shuns the company of others,* like *Diogenes* did, in ♎ *a cheerful man who is good company,* in ♏ *someone who is physically fit but squalid, poor and of an unpleasant disposition,* and in ♐ *a person who is rich and powerful but also argumentative.*

Let Saturn put on some clothes and engage in actions that are suitable and appropriate for the things we have just mentioned in accordance with the nature of the *locus* and the Sign in which he is located. Then let the sign ♐ arise, in which *Jupiter* will appear as a *celestial king held in the highest honour,* while in ♑ *he will be faint-hearted,* in ♒ *an impoverished priest,* in ♓ *a powerful man rich in both honour and wealth,* in ♈ *a general who is very lucky in battle,* in ♉ *a prisoner of Love,* in ♊ *a merchant of great sincerity,* in ♋ *a friend of princes and someone highly esteemed among the powerful,* in ♌ *wise and amiable,* in ♍ *rich in learning,* in ♎ *a Bishop, or someone rich in ecclesiastical preferment,* and in ♏ *the friend of a prince.*

Now if that part of the Zodiac which is attributed to *Aries* and in which *Mars* is known to have its dominion should ascend, then *Mars* himself will be depicted *driving a chariot with a sword in hand and lightning-bolts shooting from his eyes;* in ♉ *he will take the form of a common soldier seizing a woman,* in ♊ *he will be imitating the soul of Ulysses*[30], in ♋ *he will be rash and inconstant,* in ♌ *someone hanging or otherwise killing himself,* in ♍ *inditing letters or shooting arrows with a bow,* in ♎ *caught by Vulcan committing adultery with Venus,* in ♏ *rich in possessions,* in ♐ *the commander of an army,* in ♑ *wounding other people with a sword,* in ♒ *bold and undertaking great things,* and in ♓ *the friend of a king.*

Then if Leo should ascend and appear above the horizon with his Lord the *Sun*, then *Apollo* will have the dignity of Ruler and in ♍ will *administer justice*; in ♎ *be a merchant who carefully considers everything*; in ♏ *will fight with the Python*; in ♐ *will shoot arrows at random*; in ♑ *will be sad and gloomy*; in ♒ *will be seen navigating a river*; in ♓ *will be grappling with the ocean*; in ♈ *will be bilious and irascible*; in ♉ *will be fighting the Minotaur*; in ♊ *will be on good terms with Castor and Pollux*, and so on with the others, for if *Taurus* is rising, then it will have *Venus* in its house, who will sit on the bull's back like *Europa*, and if *Gemini* is in the ascendant then we shall have to imagine *Mercury*, and the same also with *Cancer* rising when we shall imagine the *Moon*, proceeding successively and gradually just as we have done in the above examples.

CHAPTER V
in which we discuss the secondary images.

Some people may not be comfortable with a proliferation of secondary images. To make this Art easier for such people, we can make the *loci* more distinctive by using colours, as well as by excluding certain images.

So the *first locus* will be *white* like a snow-covered meadow; the *second* will be *red*, with the image of a meadow in front of the theatre-door where a battle has taken place, so that its surface, soaked in blood, is red in colour; the *third* will be *green*, and will be an area in front of the door conspicuous for its lush grass and flourishing trees; the *fourth* will be *blue*, and will be like a valley in front of the door, watered everywhere by fountains; and the *fifth* and *last* will be an extremely gloomy underground cavern or cave, *black* in colour.

Opposite these meadows you should also imagine *five columns*, which should be similarly distinctive in shape and colour, i.e. the *two outer columns* will be *circular and round*, the *central column* will be *hexagonal*, and the *intermediate* ones *square*. They will also differ from one another in colour: these colours will correspond to those of the theatre-doors that are opposite to them, but in the opposite or reverse order, i.e. white will be facing black, and so on.

You can also attach to these columns certain rings and chains of a fantastic design, to which can be attached certain animals signifying

Adverbs, *Conjunctions*, *Prepositions* and *Interjections*, just as one might use in whole sentences.

In this case the following sequence should be used: to the *white column* attach a ring made of *silver* with a chain of the same metal; to the *red column* attach a *copper* ring with a chain made from a *tree-branch*; to the *blue* attach a *leaden ring* with a chain also made of that metal; finally, attach to the *black* column an *iron* ring with an *iron* chain.

Words acting as signifiers must however be denoted by the principal image of the idea and not otherwise, as will become apparent when you try to recall whole sentences.

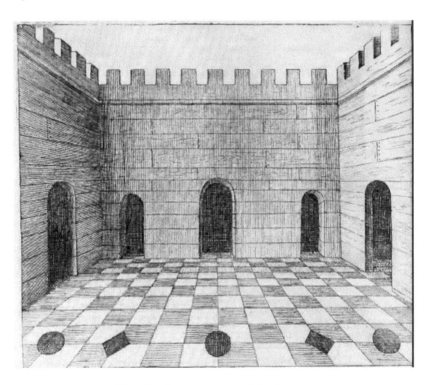

Fig. 11. *The true image of the theatre.*

CHAPTER VI

in which we discuss in how many ways principal ideas or images can be expressed in the empty loci, *both in the Round and the Square Art.*

The *actions* by which images are expressed in *loci* are usually either:	<u>Cruel</u>, i.e. someone witnessing an act of savagery, or committing a dreadful crime against the laws of nature, e.g. *a tyrant slaying someone, Lucretia committing suicide.*
	Or <u>*ridiculous*</u>, e.g. *a woman falling off a donkey and displaying her privy parts as she does so*, or anything else that makes us laugh.
	Or <u>*miraculous*</u>, e.g. *a man born with two heads*, or *a donkey teaching someone to play a stringed instrument*, or *a donkey that has actually mastered such an instrument.*
	Or <u>*repulsive and shameful*</u>, e.g. *someone acting dishonestly, or encouraging others to do so by his disgraceful behaviour.*

These actions can also be assigned to the celestial images or ideas, which we can imagine as being located in the meadows we described above.

Here again we should note that each Theatre will have five Doors, namely one *white,* one *red,* one *green,* one *blue* and one *black.* Here also you should note that you will have much greater success in this Art if, in the Zodiacal or starry sphere, you imagine historical narratives that are suited in location and action to each Sign and its *locus.*

So, for example, *corresponding to the sign of Aries* we have the story of *Jason and Medea and the Golden Fleece.* The *first idea* before the White Door will therefore be Medea on the summit of Mount Atlas gathering its magical herbs which are covered in snow. The *second,* before the Red Door, will be Medea killing her brother and hurling his limbs into the grass of the meadow. The *third* will be Medea gathering herbs in the valley of Tempe in Thessaly, abundant in brushwood and green trees, so that she can help Jason in his enterprise. The *fourth* will be Jason and Medea boarding the ship[31] with the Golden Fleece. The *fifth* will be that gloomy hovel or other place in which the bulls and the dragon, the guardians of the Golden Fleece, were bound and imprisoned by means of enchantment, and so on.

CHAPTER VII
in which we relate in how many ways 'signifying words' can be expressed in both the Round and the Square Art.

Signifying words can be expressed in three ways:	By <u>relationship</u>, i.e. when something is referred to something else, so that through that relationship it can signify something without the thing that needs to be signified actually being expressed, e.g. *ink can stand for an ink-well, blackness for ink, and a scabbard for a sword.*
	By <u>similarity</u>, i.e. when something that is expressed in a *locus* indicates something that is similar to it, e.g. *the Sirens stand for women, Henry the crowned pauper*[32] *stands for Henry King of France, etc.*
	By the <u>real presence</u>, i.e. *the image or idea of piercing someone with a sword* will stand for *a sword*. This is a case where a real thing in its nature and substance is expressed in a particular *locus* by the *action* of the image or idea.

CHAPTER VIII
in which we discuss the usefulness of expressing fixed images, which we call essential images.

If we want to make it as easy as possible to express fixed images, then we should not place anything in the middle of the *loci* that we have mentioned above, except things extracted from certain historical narratives, e.g. from the life of Julius Caesar, or that of any other Roman, or of Cleopatra, or of some Trojan, or some famous philosopher or other, or someone from Holy Scripture, such as the lives of Samson, David, Moses, Judas Maccabeus and others. The retention or memorising of historical narratives will therefore be of the greatest utility to you, as through this you may also readily memorise signifying and non-signifying words, familiar and unfamiliar words, and entire sentences, speeches and subjects.

Part III:
Treatise I, Section II, Part III, Book III
of the
Utriusque cosmi maioris scilicet et minoris

CHAPTER I
in which we discuss how many different kinds of words there are, and how the Signifying Words are explained in the various loci.

A *signifying word* is a word that can be explained in any *locus* by some vivid action of an image or idea.

A *non-signifying word* is one which cannot in itself be represented in a *locus*, due to the absence of such an action.

All *words* are either:					
	Signifying words:	*Verbs*, e.g. to kill, to dance, to sing, etc.			
		Nouns, e.g. book, sword, bull, etc.			
		Adjectives, e.g. strong, violent, sad, cheerful, etc.			
		Participles, e.g. striking, burning, falling sick, etc.			
			Less signifying, e.g	*Adverbs*, e.g. not, now.	
				Conjunctions, e.g. and, nor, and so.	
				Prepositions, e.g. through, in.	
				Interjections, e.g. oh! ah!	
		Heard			*Proper nouns*, e.g. Peter, John, Sarah, Mary, etc.
				Substantives	
	Non-signifying		*More signifying*, e.g		*Common nouns*, e.g. work, intellect, spirit, etc.
				Pronouns, e.g. who, this, that, my, etc.	
		Unheard, e.g. Gorocoga, Abricalac, Arbroc, etc.[33]			

CHAPTER II
in which we discuss the use of the Spherical Art to memorise Signifying Words.

After we have defined the *loci* and have delineated the story of Medea in the five meadows as described above, we must follow the rule we have just given in order to express the signifying words.

Suppose, for example, that I wish to denote the word *book* in the first *locus*. I will imagine Medea in the white meadow, either suspended in the ether as a subtle spirit or seated in a chariot of fire looking at a book of magic. This act of the imagination should be 'fixed' by using a real expression in the *locus* that is specific to it.

If the *second* word is *elevated*, then we can imagine the spirit of Medea looking anxiously from the top of a tower to see if her father is pursuing her.

If the *third* word is *joyful*, then we can express it by imagining the spirit of Medea rejoicing for two reasons, i.e. because of the beauty of her surroundings and partly also because there she has found herbs that are suited to her purpose.

Suppose the *fourth* word is *knife*: in that case we would persuade ourselves that Medea is throwing into the sea the knife she used to cut her brother's throat.

The *fifth* word is *light*, and to illustrate it we imagine that, in the struggle between Jason and the ever-watchful serpent and the fire-breathing bulls, an extraordinary light and an immense multitude of sparks have poured forth from the cave.

Finally, we come to the Western Theatre ♈, in the darkness of which we must gaze upon Medea's essential actions as if they were reflecting shadows.

CHAPTER III
in which we discuss the memorising of Signifying Words and their position in the Square Art.

Signifying words can be expressed in three ways: by *relationship*, *similarity*, or *real presence* or *action*.

To take an example, I can express the meaning of the word *lion* in the first door of the first *locus* by *relationship*, by imagining Samson[34] clad in a lion-skin, or alternatively by *real action* by thinking of Samson fighting the lion.

If the second word is *sword*, then I can imagine this either by *relationship*, with Delilah moved to furious wrath breaking in two her husband's scabbard which she has just found, or by *real action*, with Delilah killing herself in despair.

If the third word is *fly*, then we can imagine it by *real presence* with one of the Philistines seeking to avoid Samson's violence and fervour by seating himself on a giant fly and then rising into the air; by *relationship*, by imagining that Samson's putrefying flesh is everywhere infested with flies; or finally by *similarity*, with Samson flitting from one place to another on wings that are just like those of a fly.

CHAPTER IV

in which we discuss the memorisation in both the Arts of words that are known to us but which are either non-signifying or which signify things only with difficulty.

Substantives, adjectives and participles in the *Round Art* are usually explained by using the alphabetical sequence of the Gods, but with some action of theirs deployed around a fixed image, e.g. Neptune doing nothing or being lazy will signify 'nothingness'.

Non-signifying words are expressed using the 'alphabet of the goddesses' described above, e.g. Proserpina in great majesty can stand for the power to do something.

Pronouns are always indicated either by a vice (a monster or a demon) or by a virtue (an angel), e.g. *that* (i.e. that one over there) will be explained by a leprous monster covered in spots pointing at something with his finger.

Adverbs, Conjunctions, Prepositions and *Interjections* are signified by celestial animals. This also applies in the *Square Art*, with the exception that birds are used instead of virtues and vices.

All of these must however be conjoined with or indicated by some conspicuous action.

Sometimes we can even denote an entire animal by some distinct and conspicuous part of it, such as a *lion* by its tail, pelt or claws; an *elephant* by its teeth or by its trunk coiled backwards; a *panther* by the relationship between that animal and something with spots, as well as by its fur; a *donkey* by its lyre[35]; an *ox* by its horns; a *snake* by its venom; a camel by the garments of Saint John[36]; a *griffin* by a wing and a lion's tail; a *wild dog*[37] by its tongue or by a domesticated dog; a *rhinoceros* by its horn; a *monkey* by someone mimicking another person, or by a man who looks like a monkey; a *bear* by the constellation of the Great Bear; a *cat* by a mouse or a fire[38]; a *mule* by its burdens; a *horse* by its reins; a *lamb* by its wool; *Adam* by an apple; *Pope Boniface* by a key; *Cadmus* by a snake or tree; *David* by the head of Goliath; *Eteocles*[39] by the divided flame; *Saint Francis* by a bloodied cross; *Hercules* by a club or bow; *Jason* by the Golden Fleece or by an act of infidelity; *Midas* by gold or by golden ears of an ass; *Nestor* by a white beard; *Orpheus* by a lyre; *Prometheus* by a bloodied heart or a vulture; *Quintilian* by a grammar-book or a birch-rod; the alchemist *Raymond Lull* by a phial and an alembic; *Sinon*[40] by the Wooden Horse; *Tantalus* by hunger or by an apple-tree in the water[41]; *Ulysses* by the Sirens; and so on.

In the same way we can use an eye gazing at the Sun to represent an *eagle*[42]; darkness for a *horned owl*; blackness for a *raven*; a flying-fish for a *martin*; a man alone in the desert for a *robin*[43]; a falcon-bell for a *falcon*; a watercourse, a pointed beak or a clump of geraniums[44] for a *crane*; the roof of a house for a *swallow*; or a small snake for an *ibis*[45].

This method ensures that the object will always be carefully distinguished by the forms conceived in the Round Art, as long as the exceptions we mentioned above are respected.

CHAPTER V
in which we learn how to remember familiar proper nouns.

If you want to remember proper or common nouns that are already familiar to you, then you should allocate to the relevant *loci* other examples of the same names of people who are either personally known to you or who are familiar to you from your reading of history, in each case simply accompanied by the sort of action in which they were accustomed to engage, e.g. if I want to remember someone called *Charles* then I will allocate to the *locus* someone of that name who is well known to me, and if he is, for example, a lawyer or a notary or an ironworker etc. then he will also be engaged in this job in the *locus* where he has to be placed, using a relevant image and a conspicuous action relating to it. Alternatively, I could choose someone of that name who was famous in history, such as Charlemagne making war against the infidels, or if I wanted to remember someone called *Clement* then I would assign to my commonplace Pope Clement, perhaps holding a horn[46] in his hand for clearer distinction, and so on with other names.

CHAPTER VI
in which we learn how to remember unfamiliar proper nouns.

In this rule, *alphabetical sequences* are of the highest importance: an animal is used to signify the *first* letter, a man the *second,* an inanimate object the *third,* and a bird the *fourth,* but in each case we must not forget to assign a distinctive action to the image, which should be performing some unseemly act with the animal, man and bird.

To take an example, the Sibyl tells us[47] that the Guardian Angels are called *Heromiel, Saniel, Uriel*, etc. So in the *first locus* I will place a snake (*hydra*) which will kill the principal image of the *locus* with its venom, while on its back I will imagine the body of Eteocles on the funeral pyre holding a bowl (*labrum*) in such a way that its water puts out the fire. But the swan (*olor*) standing on his head will slake its enormous thirst by drinking up every drop of the water, so that nothing remains there except the letters *miel*, which is easy to remember once the letters *Hero* have been dropped, for *hydra* stands for H, *Eteocles* for E, *labrum* for R[48] & *Olor* for O. The related action will be that Eteocles drops dead when he touches the snake.

In the *second locus* I shall place a monkey (*simia*) which Adam is leading out of Paradise and which he is jabbing repeatedly with a pitchfork. I shall imagine that the blood flowing from the monkey is nourishing (*nutrire*) the bird known as the ibis (*ibis*).

The essential action of the image will be that the ibis should wound Adam, because he very often entered his house with the monkey and his ibis[49].

To the *third locus* I shall allocate a bear (*ursa*) onto whose back Raymond Lull (*Raimundus*) is climbing, armed with his vials and alembics. In his fury, however, the bear breaks or crushes the vials and then, in revenge, is struck by Raymond with a pestle[50].

There is, however an easier way of achieving the same result. If you wish to instantly memorise some word that you have never heard before, then you can assign to the designated *loci* certain other words (either proper nouns or signifying words) which represent all (or almost all) of the syllables of the word you have not previously heard and which you wish to remember, e.g. if you want to remember the name *Uriel*, then in the first *locus* place *Uriah the Hittite*, the man in the Second Book of Samuel who was killed in battle on David's orders. Since this term expresses two syllables of a name that you have not previously heard or been familiar with, you will imagine him being killed with a pitchfork, an object that stands for the number two. This must however be established in the right-hand part, to remind you that it stands for the first syllables, while to the left-hand part you will assign Elijah ascending to heaven holding a lance, which will stand for one syllable, and so on with the others. You can also use this technique in the Round Art.

CHAPTER VII
in which we learn how to remember whole sentences in both the Round and the Square Art.

Now that you have learned an excellent way of remembering Signifying Words, you can, if you wish to work with precision, gather together all the words in a convenient sequence in some unique place in such a way that they are kept distinct from one another.

Since, however, this would be a tedious task (and indeed, an interminable one if we had a large number of sentences), we prefer to follow a different path. In this task we should therefore obey the following rules:

First, express the perfect sense of any element through an action that is realistic and proper to it, e.g. in the sentence *'The first division of bodies is into simplicity'* you should imagine that an image is dividing certain bodies or making a division into elements that are simple.

Second, if the starting-word or initial word is non-signifying, or if it might signify something only with difficulty, then you should express that word by means of an image, as we described in Book II. The image should illustrate that action by means of the word that immediately follows. So, for example, in the case of the sentence *'Every simple motion is either straight or curved'*, Orpheus will be moved in a straight line or in a curve, or the Sun will be formed in his hand, signifying *motion* by the principle of relationship.

Third, if two or three adverbs, conjunctions and so on introduce a sentence, then that sentence should be expressed in one *locus* only, unless the following words are clearly understandable in isolation, and inseparable in sense from their antecedent.

Fourth, if you wish to distribute the said particles of the element among their *loci* you should first assign to the images certain actions of the Signifying Words that you have conceived. So, for example, if I have placed *ink* in the first *locus*, and the first element was the statement *'the form gives us the name and essence of an object'* , then I shall then imagine the ink destroying the image and will then think of the ink being wiped away to reveal the face of a beautiful girl called Maura[51].

If you want to use this technique in the Round Art, then you should use the ten doors of Medea and then of Europa, and so on.

CHAPTER VIII
in which we discuss the memorising of speeches and songs.

With speeches and songs, we follow the suggestions outlined above and use exactly the same procedure. This is easily done with songs thanks to their metrical nature.

CHAPTER IX
in which we discuss the memorisation of whole subjects, and how many different subjects are acceptable in this Art.

A *subject* in the sense in which it is understood in this context *is the perfected action of some intention which is expressed in just one* locus *either by relationship, by similarity, or even by the real presence.*

By the *perfected action* of an intention I mean that action by which the sense of some historical narrative or some wise saying or law or aphorism and so on is expressed and perfectly explained in a certain *locus.*

Since the approach varies somewhat depending on the objects in question, we shall proceed methodically and in a certain sequence.

With regard to subjects involving historical narratives, we need to know that the narrative *should be expressed in the* loci *in a twofold way*, i.e. either *generally or specifically.*

We say that a historical narrative is being expressed *generally* when its whole sequence and sense is expressed in just one *locus*, e.g. if I want to express the whole narrative of Book II of Virgil's *Aeneid* in a particular *locus*, then I can imagine the image of the *locus* on a mountain-top looking from afar while a giant wooden horse is brought into the city by night and then, still in the darkness, that same city being most deplorably set on fire on all sides.

A historical narrative is said to be expressed *specifically* when every single part of it is explained separately.

CHAPTER X

in which we explain how numerals are expressed in the loci *mentioned above.*

We have already referred to this subject in our book *De Arithmetica universali* ('On Universal Arithmetic'), where we devoted some sections specifically to the subject of 'arithmetical memory', and by this method taught a way of calculating, adding, subtracting, multiplying and dividing by means of suitable positioning in appropriate *loci* of 'memory images'. We therefore refer you to that treatise of ours[52], so that we can quickly conclude the second part of this section.

APPENDIX
Dr. Fludd on the Arithmetical Memory
Extract 1: Book X of *De Arithmetico Universali*
(from Treatise II of the Utriusque cosmi maioris scilicet et minoris)

On Memory Arithmetic.

CHAPTER I
in which we discuss the memory loci.

Rule I.
In Memory Arithmetic the location of the memory loci *must always receive special attention* in order to ensure that the lower part of the final *locus* of the square is continuously joined to the first *locus* on the right-hand side and the fourth *locus* on the left-hand side, in such a way that from three *loci* only one *locus* is formed, as will be clear from the following example.

Description of the loci *of the square according to the simple Art of Memory.*

3		2
	5	
4		1

An appropriate conversion of the loci *of the square shown above to suit the Art of Calculation.*

3	2	First sequence.
Locus for the aggregate (result) of addition, subtraction and multiplication.		

Rule II.

The above loci *will easily help you to retain in the mind a sequence of two numbers if a twofold action is established in any* locus, *but this must of course be done by proceeding from its lower part to its higher part,* as follows.

Let us imagine that we allocate to the *first* locus a man or a girl waiting for an apple or a walnut or some other kind of fruit to fall from a tree.

In the *second* locus we can imagine some people ringing bells that are suspended at the top of a very high tower.

In the *third* locus some men are eagerly hanging a fox or a wolf on a gibbet.

Please refer to Fig. 1 below to see what I mean.

Rule III.

If there are several series of additions, subtractions or multiplications at the top of this square, then three loci *of the second square should be added, filling them with a double image.*

In the *first locus*, imagine a bridge upon which a fisherman is standing, hauling quite a big fish out of the river with a hook.

Similarly, *if several* loci *are needed in these representations then you will have to connect collaterally the* loci *of one square with those of the other, either singly or doubly, just like the series of numbers to be added in the corresponding arithmetical calculations,* as shown in the following Fig. 2.

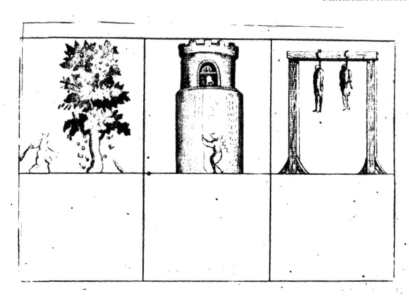

Fig. 1

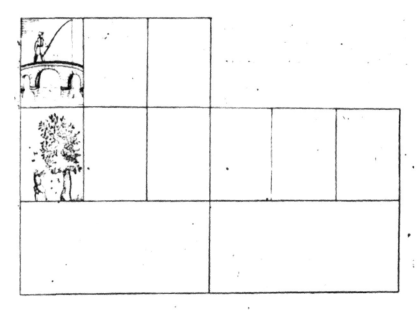

Fig. 2

CHAPTER II
On Addition

Rule I.
Suppose we need to add 164 *to* 335. Imagine a man wearing a square cap and holding a horn eagerly grasping at the fruit of a tree, who has thrust the horn towards the fruit to try to dislodge it with such violence that, under the force of the blow, the horn has shattered into minute pieces, the jagged parts of which tear his cap to shreds.

In the second *locus*, imagine a snail using his horns to injure a man ringing a bell. The bell then kills the snail by toppling a three-legged stool onto it.

In the third *locus*, imprint into your mind a wolf with a spear who is trying in various ways to cut in two the noose of a hanged man. While this is happening, the triangular gibbet topples over and frightens the wolf, causing him to flee.

Rule II.
The above images are added together by converting two images into a third.

The cap and horn of the first sequence are changed into a snake, and the snail and the triangular gibbet are changed into a dog's tail. To increase the vividness of the action the snake is allowed to become aggressive.

Similarly, in the third series of *loci*, a third metamorphosis or transmutation of the spear and the gibbet into a square book will be shown, as we can see below in Fig. 3.

CHAPTER III
On Subtraction

Rule I.
Subtraction is achieved by detaching the bases of the loci *from the upper series of* loci *and then assigning the result of the transformation to the fundamental* locus, e.g. Character 4, *a cap*, when subtracted from Character 5, *a horn*, gives us Character 1, *a spear*, and so on with the others, as is customary in conventional arithmetic.

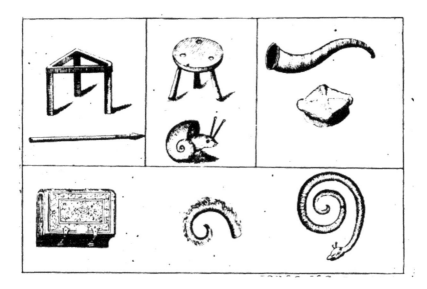

Fig. 3

CHAPTER IV

On Multiplication

In multiplication, when the multiplier is a multiple of ten then the reasoning is straightforward, but since the multiplier is sometimes conflated from many multiples of ten the fundamental *locus* must be divided into three or more equal *loci* depending on its length, of which one *locus* will be *green*, the second *white* and the third *red*, for these colour-distinctions make it easier to work out the multiplicands and display them more clearly as shown in the following example.

The aggregate (result) of the multiplication should be expressed in the black *locus*.

Multi-	plican-	ds
Multi-	pli-	ers
Green locus		
White locus		
Red locus		
Black locus		

CHAPTER V
On Division

Memory Arithmetic is very rarely used for Division, partly due to the difficulty of the concept as such, and partly because of the many operations it involves which can confuse the Memory Artist, so we are not going to discuss it here but will instead leave it to be explored by more assiduous investigators.

**Extract 2: Book I Chapter X of *De Arithmetico Universali*
(from Treatise II of the *Utriusque cosmi maioris scilicet et minoris*)**

CHAPTER X
in which we discuss the Memory Numbers.

Memory Numbers or Memory Images are:	Either <u>non-zero numerals</u>	Unity (1), such as	Spear Pestle
		Binary (2), such as	Pitchfork Pair of shears
		Ternary (3), such as	Three-legged stool Triangular gibbet
		Quaternary (4), such as	Book Square cap
		Quinary (5), such as	Sea-cucumber War-trumpet
		Senary (6), such as	Snail Retort
		Septenary (7), such as	Axe Set-square
		Octonary (8), such as	Spectacles Buttocks
		Novenary (9), such as	Coiled snake Dog's tail
	or <u>Multiples of ten</u>, expressed as:	A donkey struck by a spear A donkey shorn with shears A donkey sitting on a 3-legged stool A donkey reading a book Someone striking two donkeys with a spear	will stand for { 10 / 20 / 30 / 40 / 100
	or <u>Composites</u> of:	Either non-zero numbers only, such as	A man holding an apothecary's pestle has struck a blow with a spear = 11 An apothecary smashes a barber's shears with a pestle = 12 Peter has killed John who is sitting on a three-legged stool = 13 A barber has torn off someone's square cap and cut to pieces a snake which was biting the man = 249
		or non-zeros and multiples of ten in combination, e.g. someone has placed a book under an axe in order to chop it up, and a donkey snatching the book away to try to save it is seriously injured in the process = 470	

THE NUMERALS ILLUSTRATED
An ass will stand for zero, since (as they say) an ass is always worth absolutely nothing.

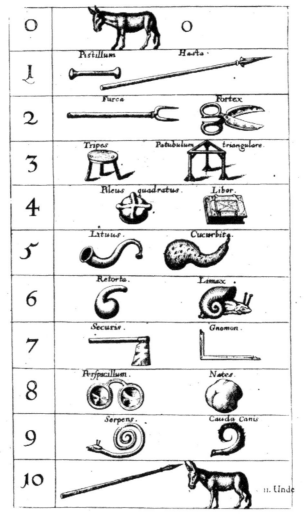

Fig. 4. The Numerals Illustrated

0 = ass; 1= pestle & spear; 2 = pitchfork & shears; 3 = three-legged stool & triangular gibbet; 4 = square cap & book; 5 = horn[53] & sea-cucumber; 6 = alchemical retort & snail; 7 = axe & set-square; 8 = spectacles & buttocks; 9 = snake & dog's tail; 10 = spear & ass.

11	Eleven will be represented by a spear with a pestle, or by two pestles or by a double-spear, and must be highlighted by appropriate actions.
9136	This number can be memorised by thinking of a snake being pursued by a man with a spear who, in his pursuit, passes through triangular gibbet and then kills with the spear a snail climbing up the gibbet.
2000	Even this kind of number can be intentionally expressed by imagining three donkeys with their mouths open pursuing and threatening a man carrying a pitchfork. A similar procedure can be followed for all other numbers.

Rule I.

To instil some variety, we suggest using two images for each of the non-zero numbers, as two numbers of the same kind are often found together and if these are expressed together simultaneously in the memory *loci* then they would undoubtedly confuse the Artist, for 'the memory is always refreshed by diversity'.

The numbers 224 or 111, for example, should not be expressed by two pitchforks or by three spears respectively, as several similar images simply confuse the representations which have been impressed in the memory.

Rule II.

Memory Numbers should always be highlighted in the relevant loci *by means of a vivid action.* This will help them to be retained in the mind longer and more securely.

Rule III.

A Memory Number should sometimes be expressed by means of a relationship, e.g. if a binary number has to be designated then we can think of a barber all by himself without his scissors, along with an appropriate action. If the number is unary then we think of a soldier, and if ternary an executioner, for a barber's reference will be to scissors, a soldier to a spear, and an executioner to a triangular gibbet.

Rule IV.

The true sequence of images will always follow the sequence of actions, i.e. the principal agent will occupy the first *locus* counting from the left, while the immediate victim of his action will be the second agent, who will claim for himself the second *locus*, and so on, e.g. if the number 48 has to be memorised then let a physician be dressed in a square cap which falls off and strikes his spectacles (in the second *locus*) which causes them to be shattered.

TRACTATUS PRIMI.
SECTIONIS II.
PORTIO III.
LIBER I.

De animæ memorativæ Scientia,
quæ vulgo ars memoriæ
vocatur.

CAP. I.
De Auctoris industria in comparando & excolendo
artem memoriæ in exoticis regionibus.

Cum ego in peregrinationibus meis regnum Galliæ inter alia præcipue ultro citroque perlustrarem. *Nemosiensem* tandem civitatem, invitatus fama, extantium in ea antiquitatum petebam, ubi apud quendam ex arte sua memoriæ satis famigerabilem cœpi primum illius artis suavitatem degustare: Mox deinde in urbe *Avenione* ad flumen Rhodani sita hanc artem ærumnabili labore, nullo penitus Magistro præeunte eam aggressus, incolui. Cum itaque in ejus exercitio magis expertus evaderem, a nonnullis Galliæ Principibus, tam hujus artis gratia, quam cæterarum scientiarum mathematicarum ratione in multos locos Provinciæ accersitus fui a *Marchione* scilicet *Orizontis, Vicecomite Cadinetæ, Episcopo Rhiensi*, quem principem illius loci magnum esse perhibebant. At ego tandem, reliquis, & iis quidem magnis promissis recusatis *Marcelliam* perveni: ubi *Ducem Guisiensem* & fratellum ejus *Laurenæ Principes*, atque hunc Mitilenæ militem, insignis indolis & gratiosi corporis juvenem artes mathematicas docere cœpi, atque inter cæteras quoque artem istam juveni proposui; Qui certe miro modo scientiarum capax brevissimo temporis intervallo ita pollebat cognitione, ut cæteris nobilibus; qui ibi aderant, scientia brevi temporis spatio præcelleret: *Nemosii* igitur primum, mox *Avignione*, denique *Aquæsextiis*, & ultimo Marcelliis hujus scientiæ penetralia pro virili mea pervestigando, aliquid in ea vidi & didici: Quod quale quale sit: tibi illud (lector) libentissime gratis offero, quod mihi & pretio & labore haud exiguo constitit.

CAP. II.
Memoria quid & quotuplex? specierumque utriusque memoriæ retinendarum ratio.

Antequam hujus artis aream ingrediamur inprimis necessarium existimamus scire, quid sit illud, circa quod hæc ars versatur, & methodice in hoc nostro tractatu progrediamur. *Est* igitur *memoria fidelissima receptorum & imaginum, seu rerum, quarum species intellectu sunt perceptæ, custos atque conservatrix*: vel *est habitus quidam referens species post aliquantulum temporis lapsum quarum objectum semper est præteritum.* Et quoniam de memoria hic agitur, quæ tam hominibus, quam brutis communis est, intelligere lectorem velim, quod hominis memoria differat a memoriæ brutorum in eo, quod hæc tantum est sensitiva, recipiens duntaxat sensibilia, rerum phantasmata, illa vero intellectiva & sensitiva simul. His igitur diligenter observatis, ad memoriæ intellectualis species sic procedendum putamus, ut demonstremus, eam *duplici modo* considerandam esse, videlicet, *vel* prout in naturali sua dispositione accipitur, cujus naturam in definitione superiori explicuimus; *vel* quatenus artis adjumento refertur & dicitur *memoria artificialis*, quoniam artis illius præceptis coadjuvatur, quæ memorativa appellatur. *Memoriam* ergo *artificialem* definimus, esse *memoriæ naturalis per artem* (in ficta imaginationis operatione positam) *inventæ operationem.* Unde liquet, quod memoria artificialis per se non plus faciat sine memoriæ naturalis præsentia, quam cyphra arithmetica absque digiti præsentia. Harum vero memoriæ specierum retinendarum ratio est varia, quatenus una veritatum imagines retinet, prout sunt, altera per species fictas & imaginatione conceptas, naturalis memoriæ imperfectionem adjuvat. Dicunt ergo Medici, quod specierum memoriæ naturalis retentio fiat per contractionem alicujus vermis, vel carunculæ vermiformis in medio cerebri constitutæ: illarumque iterum amissionem ex ejusdem vermis diductione seu extensione provenire ferunt: At vero memoriæ artificialis retentio fieri solet per assiduam phantasiæ actionem, vanis & fictis idæis ac iconibus veritatis species myrothecio memoriæ imprimentem: Id quidem quod accidere solet, propter imaginationis propinquitatem & vicinitatem actionis ejus ad cellulam memoriæ, quæ quidem cum recens & continua sit facta, assidue quasi pulsat memoriam, & veluti viva actione (licet speciebus fictis ac inanimatis facta) pulsando speciem retinendam subinde memoriæ objicit, non secus atque cum mutus aliquis per signa loco verborum alicui rem quandam indicare & declarare studet.

CAP. III.
An qua via alia quam sola virtute phantastica comparari vel includi possit memoria artificialis.

Agnoscimus, memoriam naturalem non nisi duplici via posse adjuvari, videlicet aut *assidua phantasticæ facultatis operatione*; quæ per rerum fictarum repræsentationem veritatum impressiones inscribit memoriæ, aut *virtute medicamentorum* labefactatam memoriam naturalem reficientium. Phantasia enim res fictas meatui vermiformem carunculam continenti offerente, ipsa eas sua dilatatione introducit ad rationalem cellulam, ut ibi rationaliter perpendantur, a qua illæ ulterius ad memoriæ conclave e vestigio mittuntur, ut in ejus specu, contrahente sese vermiformi caruncula, custodiantur. Medicamenta quoque conferunt memoriæ diminutæ, aut præter naturam læsæ, sive illud fiat ob frigidatis & humiditatis copiam & exuberantiam, sive ob caliditatis & siccidatis excessum. Imo vero imaginatio ipsa etiam harum qualitatum præter naturæ leges prædominio læditur, & læsa medicamentis restauratur atque in integrum suum statum reducitur: De quibus medici abunde tractaverunt. Ultra autem hos duos memoriam debilem adjuvandi modos non noverunt alios Physici & Medici, præter unicum illud supernaturaliter electis quandoque concessum donum, quod gratia & splendore divino illis extraordinarie inspiratur.

CAP. IV.
De duplici phantasiæ actione circa memoriam artificialem versante.

Phantasia ad completam artis memoriæ perfectionem operatur dupliciter; videlicet *aut idæis*, quæ proprie sunt formæ a rebus corporeis separatæ, cujusmodi sunt spiritus, umbræ, animæ, &c. similiter Angeli, de quibus præcipue in *arte nostra rotunda* agemus. Nec enim vocabulo ideæ hic utimur tali modo, quo *Plato*, qui eam pro Dei mente accipere solebat, sed pro re qualibet ex quatuor elementis non composita, videlicet, pro re alia simplici in ætherea mundi parte vel spirituali per imaginationem concepta; Verbi gratia, pro Angelis, Dæmonibus, stellarum effigiebus,

& Deorum vel Dearum imaginibus, quibus cœlestia attribuuntur, & quæ magis de natura spirituali participant, quam de corporali; similiter pro virtutum & vitiorum in imaginatione conceptis & effictis umbris, quæ etiam pro Dæmonibus sunt habendæ. Atqui si discipuli ingenium nequeat hujuscemodi idæarum figuras conceptui imprimere, electiones suas facere potest inter bruta, homines, & res inanimatas sensui obvias ac occurrentes, atque earum imagines in cœli partibus concipere loco umbrarum & idæarum. Aut operatur phantasia *imaginibus rerum corporalium*, quæ quidem, tametsi, modo phantastico percipiuntur, non tamen ut res incorporeæ considerantur, sed a corporali actione depictæ atque a sola imaginatione fictæ; Exempli causa, si imaginemur, lupum interficere aliquem agnum, Petrum equestrem spatham præacutam mucrone infesto devorare, serpentem virulentum lubricis amplexibus tibiæ cujusdam hominis bene tibi noti inhærere, &c. Nam sola imaginatione & modo phantastico res sensibiles considerare debet artifex, videlicet ita res illas in phantasia figurare, ut pictor peritus res visibiles coloribus vivis depingere & exornare solet. Ex his igitur videmus, quod memoria solummodo artificialiter corrigi possit aut medicamentis, aut phantasiæ operatione versante vel circa idæas, quæ proprie ad *artem rotundam* pertinent vel circa imagines rerum corporalium, quæ *arti quadratæ* magis conveniunt. Quare eos, haud sibi constare putamus, qui artem aliquam memoriæ sine medicamentorum aut phantasiæ operatione esse volunt, & confidenter credunt. Quod quidem inde oritur, quoniam aut in Philosophia naturali omnino rudes sunt; aut a verbosis nebulonibus & impostoribus ad illam opinionem seducti decipiuntur, existimantes esse in rerum natura artem memoriæ, quæ omnibus idæis & imaginibus relictis queat addisci. Hujusmodi quidem farinæ erat quidam *Jurisconsultus Aquæsextiæ*, qui audacter affirmabat, se quendam in civitate *Tolosæ* vidisse, qui se exactam memoriæ artem virtute annuli aut virgulæ Salomoni attributæ, comparasse asseruerit: quod quidem si unquam factum fuit, modis naturalibus factum fuisse penitus negamus: Virtute tamen præstigiosa fortasse Dæmonum, vel metaphysica Spiritus Sancti influentia tale quid vere & infallibiliter posse contingere concedimus: Attamen necesse est etiam, ut phantasia in actu metaphysico concurrat ad complendam rei naturalis perfectionem; quoniam phantasia est quasi ostium sive porta memoriæ, per quam necesse est ut omnes species sensibiles, quæ memoriæ conclavi custodiri debent, ingrediantur.

CAP. V.

Utrum memoria commodius exprimatur in arte rotunda vel quadrata.

Ars nostra *Sphærica* procul dubio est multo commodior, tum ratione capacitatis figuræ, quæ est rotunda, & per consequens magis ad opus utilis, tum quia quilibet sphæræ locus, partitionem suam naturalem possidet in qualibet mundi sphæra: Porro etiam quælibet sphæra situm & positionem suam naturalem habet absque ulla suæ positionis alteratione: Unde certus est operator, quod locos suos invariabiles semper speculetur: similiter nullus Planeta extra suum orbem movere aut deviare cognoscitur, sed sua operatione, actu & dominio semper in sua propria sphæra fruitur: Ars ergo hæc nostra sphærica memoriam Microcosmi naturalem mirifice adjuvare, & in quam plurimis, ratione respectus ejus, quem ad Microcosmi partes & actiones habet, multum certe præstare potest. In *quadrata* autem *arte* nihil naturale invenitur, videlicet nec locus, nec partitiones, nec imagines: Et tamen quadrata communia (quæ *loci* hujus artis *communes* nuncupantur) Astronomiæ imperitis magis conferunt quam altera, quatenus aulæ, conclavis aut cubiculi quadrati species facilius imprimuntur hominum literarum ignarorum conceptui, quam idææ sola contemplatione consideratæ: Atque hinc fit, ut ars ista quadrata a majori hominum parte præferatur arti rotundæ: quamvis hæc sit illa longe dignior, & naturæ magis consona; illa vero arti magis familiaris, & sensibus subjectior.

CAP. VI.

De insigni nonnullorum in hac arte versantium, errore, & præ cæteris illi refelluntur, qui palatiis imaginariis utuntur.

Aliqui in hac arte versati voluerunt artem suam quadratam collocare in palatiis noviter imaginationis inventione fabricatis seu extructis: Quam autem inconveniens sit hæc illorum opinio breviter explicabimus: Si enim imaginationis seu phantasiæ operationes inprimis scientiæ opticæ comparaverimus, videbimus rem istam longe aliter sese habere: Nam si multa specula ita sibi ad invicem applicuerimus, ut alicujus in speculo primo visi objecti imago a primo illo speculo in secundum, & iterum imago illa in secundo speculo visa in tertium reflectatur, atque illa ulterius imago speculi tertii in quartum, & sic in cæteris, percipiemus equidem imaginem speculi primi esse clariorem, perspicuiorem, &

completiorem imagine speculi secundi, & hanc secundi illa tertii, & sic in quarto & quinto, ita ut ultima imaginis reflexio tandem obscura admodum & vix perceptibilis futura sit, id sane, quod fit propter debilitatem radiorum fractorum in multiplicatione reflexionum, ita ut prima reflexio sit fortior secunda, & secunda tertia, & sic in cæteris: Sic etiam dicimus, quod quo magis in hac arte opifex penetrat in phantasmatis penetralia, eo debiliores evadant imaginariarum ejus iconum effigies: Et per consequens, magis manca atque deficiens erit imaginationis operativa virtus. Ex quibus sequitur, quod quo propinquius & magis immediate procedit imaginationis similitudo a realitate sensus, eo sit in hac arte certior, validior, durabilior & efficacior. Atqui prædictæ farinæ homines conantur petere fundamentum suæ operationis non a realitate, sed a chimæra quasi & figmento rei, quæ nunquam extitit in rerum natura, ac si secundum prædictæ opticæ operationem, crederemus primi speculi imagine non visa, nec a veritate & realitate derivata, eandem tamen in speculo secundo aut tertio conspici posse, quod quidem absurdum est & impossibile: Non ergo erit conveniens nova palatia fingere, quæ nunquam extiterunt uspiam, quoniam talis artificis fictio seducet mentem ejus a veritatis contemplatione, sed realis sit domus, aut castellum vel palatium, ut a loco communi sensibus suis bene cognito, tanquam fundamento opus tuum struendo, certiori ordine progrediaris: Etenim si fundamentum e memoria tollatur aut elabatur, totum corpus peribit, & subito evanescet: Quod quidem facillime fieri potest, si fictus sit primus locus communis: At vero in re sensibus obvia non est ullus talis accidentis timor, aut etiam, si quid tale forsan eveniat, locus iterum visus de facili rursus in memoriam redibit. Porro etiam, ut in speculorum reflexionibus dictum est, quo longius in multiplicatione rerum conceptarum distat earum imago a fundamento, eo debilior erit ejus impressio in memoria: Quare maxima erit fixionis prolongatio, primum imaginari palatium, deinde cubicula istius vel illius coloris, figuræ rotundæ, &c. postea quodlibet eorum latus in quinque[54] partes dividere, ac mox quamlibet partitionem figuris etiam inventis implere, atque ultimo loco res retinendas iis aliqua actione imprimere: oblivione autem submerso palatio, reliqua etiam, videlicet cubicula, eorumque loci, & imagines, ac res memorandæ penitus auferentur. Præterea, quam debilis erit ille actus (qui præcipuum & primum locum obtinet in hac arte) cujus vivacitate res in memoria conservari debent, tum quatenus ejus fundamentum est fictum, tum etiam, quatenus a veritatis fundamento per integrum gradum in fixione recedit. Denique hujus rei rationem redarguit etiam illud in medicina experimentum: etiamsi calculo vesicæ laborantibus, medicamentum satis validum per os adhibeatur; attamen, quia in itinere suo illud gradatim aliquid de proprietate sua perdit, partem illius ventriculo, partem jecori et sanguini, & partem renibus relinquendo, fit inde, ut illud ita debile sit cum in vesicam permeat, ut parum aut nihil fere ejus in suo officio præstare valeat, cujus gratia corpori infusum erat: simili itaque modo etiam imaginationis actus in multiplicatione inventionis unius super aliam subinde evadet debilior. Et proinde concludimus, *quod a realibus incipiat & procedat phantasiæ operatio non ab intentionalibus*, quoniam fortiores, certiores, & veritati propinquiores sunt actus ab iis egredientes, et in iis reconditi.

CAP. VII.
Contra illos, qui bruta solummodo, eaque firmiter in locis communibus utriusque artis collocant.

Equidem non possumus in hac arte pro peritis habere eos, qui bruta, sive animalia irrationalia locis palatii sive domus & cubiculorum ejus imprimere solent, quamvis id faciant secundum alphabeti ordinem attribuendo scilicet asinum primo loco, bovem secundo, &c. Etenim hæc ipsa, quatenus bruta sunt, non possunt explicare rem sive actum rationalem & soli homini proprium: Quare imaginis irrationalitas erit fortasse in causa, ut subjecti rationalis obliviscatur artifex propter impossibilitatem actionis, quæ bestiæ attribuitur; verbi gratia, si oratorem velim in primo loco imprimere asino, debemus imaginari asinum more oratoris vestitum cum libro in manu et pileo in capite: Quod quidem omnino absurdum videbitur rationi, qua gubernatur homo; quia asino nec sunt vestimenta, nec liber, nec manus. Quocirca melius & rectius esse existimamus, ut imagines rationales dictis locis assignemus, cum nulla sit actio sive belluina sive humana, quam non queat homo luculenter sua actione exprimere, sive imitando, sive partes suas proprias agendo: si igitur asinum velimus exprimere, possumus imaginari, quod hominis imago in loco fixa insiliat dorso asini, aut doceat asinum artem legendi, &c.

CAP. VIII.
Contra illos, qui ad species imaginabiles retinendas locis vacuis utuntur.

Sunt etiam nonnulli in hac arte versati, qui in errorem adhuc majorem incidunt, imo vero contra naturæ leges insurgere videntur: quoniam viam adhuc difficiliorem, quam illi, quorum in præcedentibus mentionem fecimus, sequuntur, methodoque deteriori utuntur. Namque hi ipsi tam longe recedunt ab errore superiorum, ut loca vacua usurpando nihil omnino illis imprimant: sed res memoriæ mandandas in iis nudis & intectis reponunt, inculcando frequens illud Philosophorum axioma; *Frustra fit per plura, quod fieri potest per pauciora*: Sed possem etiam ita inferre, frustraneam & inutilem esse Tetrachordi, Pentachordi, Hexachordia in musica inventionem, quoniam tota musicæ dimensio in Monochordo reperitur: Et tamen qui musicæ sunt periti, faciliorem & pleniorem eam inveniunt in polichordo quam in monochordo: simili itaque modo etiam non negamus artem memoriæ fieri posse ex locis vacuis; attamen a perfectione & facilitate artis hoc longius distare atque difficilius a discipulo apprehendi dicimus. Præterea etiam certum est quod nulla sit inter locos distinctio, nisi figura aliqua seu imago figura phantastica distincta cuilibet eorum imprimatur: Unde hic eorum error errorum atque confusionem in hac arte haud exiguam pariet. Et proinde necesse erit, si illud evitare velimus, ut imagines distinctas cuilibet loco assignemus, ne confusio & absurditas in hac arte suboriatur, cum earum præsentia quilibet locus ab alio quam optime distinguatur.

CAP. IX.
De loco communi artis rotundæ, deque ejus partitione in propriis locis pro vocabulorum recordatione.

Locus communis artis rotundæ est pars mundi ætherea, scilicet orbes cœlestes, numerando ab octava sphæra, & finiendo in sphæra Lunæ. Partitionem autem ejus *duplicem* fecimus; *unam* scilicet *ratione loci & ordinis* qua eum naturaliter primum secundum Zodiaci distinctionem in duodecim æquales partes distribuimus, quas signa cœlestia Astrologi vocaverunt; *Alteram* vero *ratione temporis*, in qua fit subdivisio: Nam, quia primum mobile, cursum suum raptum uno die naturali perficit (ab oriente nempe in occidentem) idcirco quæ libet diei hora respondet quinque Zodiaci gradibus, quod quidem spatium est dimidia signi pars. Signi autem longitudo delineat motum Solis quantitate unius horæ diei. Peracto Zodiaco vel octava sphæra incipiendum cum cœlo Saturni, & sic in cæteris peripheria cœli medii versus sphæram ignis descendendo, ut in figura sequenti explicatur.

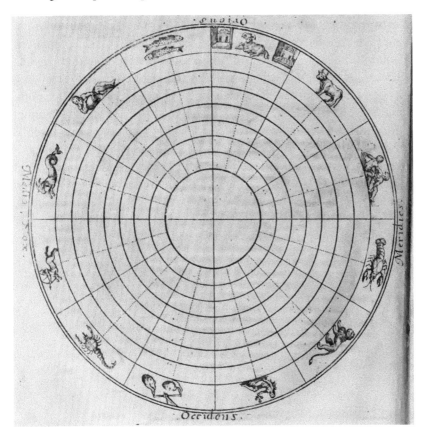

Loci iterum *temporales* sunt *duplices*, cum *alius* sit orientalis, qui scilicet in eodem signo orientalem mundi plagam respicit, atque hunc locum theatro albo impleri imaginabimur: *Alius* vero *occidentalis*, sive occidentalis signi portio, in qua ponetur theatrum quoddam nigrum, de quo postea dicemus.

CAP. X.
De theatri orientalis & occidentalis descriptione.

Theatrum appello illud, in quo omnes vocabulorum, sententiarum, particularum orationis seu subjectorum actiones tanquam in theatro publico, ubi comœdiæ & tragœdiæ aguntur, demonstrantur. Hujusmodi theatrorum *speciem unam* in puncto orientis sitam esse imaginabimini; quæ realis seu corporea, sed quasi vapore æthereo consideranda erit: Sitque illa theatri umbra similitudinibus spirituum agentium repleta. *Primum* ergo theatrum habebit colorem album, lucidum & splendidum, præ se ferens diem, diurnasque actiones. Quare in oriente collocabitur, quia Sol ab Oriente se attollens diem incipit, claritatemque mundo pollicetur: *Secundum* vero fingetur imbutum colore nigro, fusco & obscuro: illudque in Occidente positum imaginaberis, quia Sol in Occidente existens noctem & obscuritatem brevi venturam denunciat. Quodlibet autem horum theatrorum habebit *quinque portas* ab invicem distinctas, & fere æquidistantes, quarum usus postea demonstrabimus.

CAP. XI.

De loco communi artis quadratæ, deque ejus in locos convenientes divisione; similiter de cubiculorum electione & dispositione pro hujus artis opere.

Communis hujus artis locus erit conclave sive cubiculum, cujus latera sint æqualiter quadrata aut parallela: Nec erit hujusmodi cubiculum fictum aut imaginatione sola conceptum, secundum illorum intentionem, qui palatia mente concipere solebant, quia confusio inde sequeretur, & obscuritas in phantasiæ operationibus vim actionis obruentibus: Quare necessarium existimamus, ut cubicula realia eligantur, & ea quidem talia, quæ ornatu, pulchritudine prospectu, aut re aliqua oculo sint jucunda, atque ut ab invicem optime distinguantur: super portam autem cujusque cubiculi depingatur historia aliqua insignis, uti (verbi gratia) Herculis hydram interficientis, Cerberum prosternentis, aut Medeæ fratrem jugulantis, aut Actæonis in cervum conversi, & hujusmodi aliæ: Sintque omnes istiusmodi historiarum imagines extrinsecus super ostia conclavium descriptæ: Locorum vero internorum, qui & minus communes dicuntur, ordines, eorumque partitione & partium subdivisiones methodi melioris gratia in sequentem distinctionem redegimus.

	Externus, in quo imagines super portam extrinsecus ad completiorem cubiculi unius ab altero distinctionem, quasi nomine suo proprio exprimuntur.			
Locus est <u>duplex</u>, scilicet		*Commune*, qui sunt *sex*, scilicet	*Quatuor latera cubiculi quadrata.* *Basis seu terra.* *Tectum seu cubiculi cœlum.*	
	Internus, qui subdividitur in *locos*.			
			Minus proprii, ut sunt *duo parallelogrammata exteriora*, nempe 1. & 3.	
		Non communes, qui sunt vel		
			Magis proprii, ut sunt	*Quatuor partes quadratæ parallelorum extremorum subdivisæ in 1. 2. 3. 4.* *Parallelogrammum in medio.*

Primum igitur a latere dextro ad portæ introitum incipere solemus, quoniam talis debet esse artificis motus, qualis est diurnus motus Solis, qui cursum suum incipit a dextra cœli parte atque in sinistram mundi partem decurrit, videlicet ab Oriente in Occidentem: Non bene itaque aut methodice operantur illi, qui a sinistro latere incipiunt, prætendentes quod talem motum observare soleamus in scribendo. Verum enimvero convenit arti in omnibus suis actionibus semper imitari naturam.

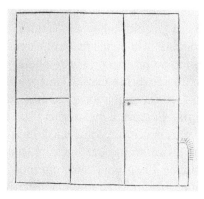

Quadrati figura.

Divisione ergo & subdivisione facta & duobus parallelogrammatibus extremis in duas partes æquales divisis, prima parallelogrammatis basis erit primi cubiculi locus, & pars ei supereminens erit secundus: Summitas autem parallelogrammatis secundi erit tertius locus: quartus vero erit ejus basis: Et totum tertium parallelogramma in medio situm erit quintus & ultimus locus ejusdem lateris: Quare 6. latera quadrata per 5. multiplicata dabunt 30. locos hujus arti necessarios. Atque ita debes in omnibus aliis lateribus dividendo & subdividendo procedere, quemadmodum fecisti in primo.

CAP. XII.

Quam figuram debeamus unicuique horum locorum dare?

Pro majori conformitate dabimus unicuique horum prædictorum locorum, figuram theatri, continentis 3. portas, in cujus medio erit imago fixa, quam essentialem appellamus; quæ tamen per accidens aliquando cogitur decedere ex loco suo proprio in aliquem exteriorum, uti apparebit in sequentibus.

Forma Theatri.

De animæ memorativæ scientia.

CAP. I.

De Alphabetis quibusdam necessariis ad vocabulorum, sententiarum,
orationum & subjectorum in memoria retentionem
& præsertim in arte rotunda.

In utraque arte *rotunda* scilicet & *quadrata* requiruntur *quinque ordines*
alphabetici: quorum *unus* erit virorum, *alter* fœminarum, *tertius*
brutorum, *quartus* avium & *quintus* piscium. Viri autem qui considerandi
veniunt in arte sphærica debent esse vel Dii vel spiritualia hominum
corpora astris dedicata, qui fingi debent ab omnibus corporibus
elementaribus immunes. Atque hoc idem quoque de fœminis naturæ
cœlestis est intelligendum. Nomina autem Deorum & cum Diis
viventium sunt hi; *Apollo* cum radiis solaribus, *Bacchus* cum uvis,
Cupido cum arcu et pharetra, *Dæmogorgon* qui & *Pluto* Deus infernalis,
Æolus, Faunus, Ganymedes, Hymenæus, Jupiter, Lucifer, Mars,
Neptunus, Orion, Pan, Quirinus, Romulus, Saturnus, Titan, Vulcanus.
Nomina vero Dearum & fœminarum cœlestium sunt illa, *Andromache,*
Bellona, Ceres, Diana, Europa, Flora, Gorgon, Hyades, Juno, Lucina,
Minerva, Natura, Opis, Proserpina, Quinquatria, Rumia, Thetis, Venus.
Porro nomina brutorum hæc sunt *Aries, Bos, Caprinus, Delphin, Equus,*
Felis, Gorgoneus serpens, Hydra, Iricinus, Leo, Mulus, Nereus, Onager,
Pegasus volans, Questor, Rhinoceros, Scorpius, Taurus, Ursa. Ad aves
autem quod attinet, quia in universa sphæra octava tres tantum, aves
reperiuntur videlicet *Aquila, vultur & corvus,* idcirco earum ordinem in
spiritus mutabimus virtutis aut vitii alicujus specimen induentes. Sic
considerabitur *Ambitio* extensis alis sursum spectans, *Bestialitas* pilis
repleta deorsum prospiciens, *Crudelitas* cum ense sanguinolento in una
manu & cor transfossum tenens manu altera, *Desperatio* se ipsam
suspendens, *Ebrietas* Cyathum vino repletum tenens, *Fortitudo*
columnæ innitens seu columnam amplectens, *Gula* ventre extenso
semper comedens, *Humilitas* genibus flexis, *Infamia* sordide maculis
ubique contaminata, *Lætitia* læto seu hilari vultu & floribus coronata

canens aut saltans, *Miseria* pannis obsita & morbo tabescens, *Nemesis* manibus sanguinolentis, *Obedientia humilitate* statu minata, *Pudicitia* albis induta vestimentis, *Querela* iracundiæ flammis percita, *Religio* crucem manu tenens, *Spes* anchoram cæruleam tenens, *Timor* currens & semper retrospiciens, *Verecundia* corona aurea exornata, *Zelotypia* clam observans aliorum actiones. Porro rerum inanimatarum & ipsorum numerorum ordines ipsis rerum figuris seu similitudinibus exprimuntur, uti in sequentibus duobus ordinibus patet.

Oportet autem imaginari hæc omnia esse quasi umbras & res transparentes seu corpora diaphana in regione ætherea apparentia.

CAP. II.

De alphabetis & nominibus pro arte quadrata.

Imagines in hac arte considerandæ sunt, uti se habent in natura elementari, hoc est, ut sint quodammodo corporeæ, licet tenui & subtili modo. Virorum, autem alphabetum sumitur ab illis, qui bene tibi sunt cogniti; aut etiam poteris pro libitu ex historiis tibi aliquas personas deligere: sed longe melius erit uti illis, qui cogniti tibi sunt aut familiares; Exempli gratia, *Abraham, Bernhardus, Carolus, Daniel, Emanuel, Franciscus, Guilielmus, Henricus, Johannes, Laurentius, Matthæus, Nicolaus, Oliverius, Petrus, Quintilianus, Richardus, Salomon, Thomas, Vincentius.* Si ex historiis, *Achilles, Brutus, Cadmus, Diogenes, Eteocles, Fabius, Ganymedes, Hercules, Jason, Leander, Midas, Nestor, Orion, Prometheus, Quintilianus, Romulus, Sinon, Tantalus, Ulysses* cum Circe, *Xerxes* cum exercitu, *Yxion* rota contusus. Fœminarum tibi notarum nomina hæc erunt; *Agrippina, Barbara, Catharina, Dalia, Elisabetha, Francisca, Guliana, Hester, Jana, Laurina, Martha, Nerea, Oriana, Paulina, Quirina, Rosamunda, Sara, Tomisena, Valeriana.* Historica autem fœminarum nomina erunt illa, *Ariadne, Bersabe, Clitemnestra, Dido, Europa, Flora, Galilæa, Helena, Jana, Lais, Medea, Niobe, Olympias mater Alexandri, Penelope, Quintiliana, Roxana, Semiramis, Tomyris, Vesta.* Nomina brutorum hæc sunt, *Asinus, Bos, Camelus, Dama, Elephas, Felis, Gryphus, Hydra, Jumentum, Leo, Mulus, Nereus serpens magnus, Ovis, Panthera, Questor* bestia latrans instar canis, *Rhinoceros* habens cornu in fronte, *Simia, Tigris, Ursa.* Nomina avium erunt illa: *Aquila, Bubo, Corvus, Drepanus, Erithacus* avis sola manens, *Falco, Grus, Hirundo, Ibis, Luscinia, Milvus, Noctua, Olor, Pica,*

Querquedula, Regulus, Sturnus, Turdus, Vespertilio. Vide figuras Num. 3. & 4.

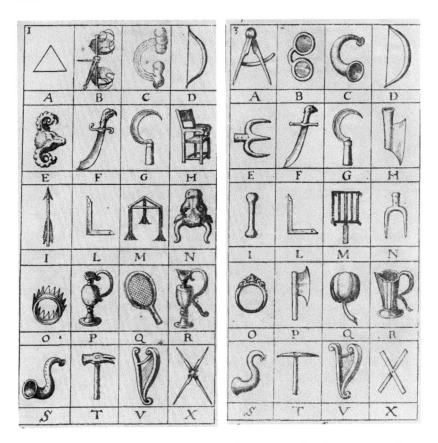

Ordo Alphabeticus rerum inanimatarum.

Figuræ rerum inanimatarum pro hac arte.

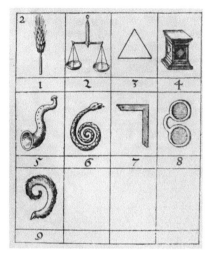 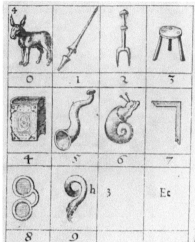

Ordo Characterum Arithmeticorum in hac arte.

Characteres Arithmetici in hac arte.

Et sic in cæteris: Nam homo insidens dorso asini & lanceam manu tenens significabit 10. Cum furca vero 20. cum tripode 30. cum libro 40. & sic in cæteris. Atque si 11. in loco aliquo volueris phantastico modo consignare, duos homines, duas lanceas gerentes imaginaberis: Quod si 432. volueris exprimere, finges hominis imaginem a parte sinistra librum manu tenere, in sinistra[55] vero parte imaginaberis pistorem aut agricolam furca instructum, & in medio constitues fœminam tripodi insidentem assignatis, scilicet, cuique harum personarum convenientibus actionibus.

CAP. III.
Quotuplex sit hujus artis idæa, & quibus actionibus assignanda in quolibet sphæræ loco.

Idæa seu *imaginaria* *forma* hujus artis est	Aut *principalis*, quæ scilicet in omni vocabulo principali, aut particula membri alicujus orationis vel sententiæ agit: Eritque Arietis effigies in primo loco primi orbis: At si actio vocabuli prædominantis non sufficiat ad expressionem rei significandæ, tunc potest adjuvari actionibus domini ejusdem signi, scilicet Martis: sed hoc raro accidit.
	Aut *minus principalis*; cum nempe ad insigniorem distinctionem historia in orientali signi theatro, naturæ signi imprimitur: Sit ergo *Jason* in primo loco collocatus, vellus aureum manu tenens, *Medea* in secundo, *Paris* pastor in tertio, *Daphne* in quarto, & *Phœbus* in quinto significans diurnam esse constellationem & masculam: atque sic in cæteris *theatris orientalibus*.

In *theatris* vero *occidentalibus* debemus solummodo imaginari umbras formarum primi theatri obscuro modo apparentes; quia hujus theatri color, quatenus noctis est principium, fuscus apparere solet phantasiæ oculis.

CAP. IV.
De ordine principali idæarum per sphæras Planetarum.

Per universam Saturni sphæram ordo principalis erit talis: Primus hujus sphæræ locus ascendens erit *Capricornus*, & sic consequenter secundum signorum successionem: quatenus Capricornus est Saturni domus diurna. *Saturnus* itaque in ♑. *rex ditissimus*, in ♒. *Senex prudentissimus & dux*, in ♓. *piscator*, in ♈. *iratus & invidus*, in ♉. *lubricus & luxuriosus*, in ♊. *balbutiens sed tamen doctissimus & prudentissimus*, in ♋. *mercator melancholicus ex damno*, in ♌. *fortunatus senex & nobilis*, in ♍. *sagax*,

sed hominum societatem fugiens, ut *Diogenes*, in ♎. *homo jucundus &
bonus socius*, in ♏. *homo vitalis, squalidus, pauper & virulentæ
dispositionis*, in ♐. *dives & potens sed contentiosus*: Induat ergo
Saturnus vestimenta, habeatque actiones aptas & convenientes rebus
prædictis, pro loci & signi natura, in quo reperitur. Deinde oriatur signum
♐. ubi *Jupiter* apparebit tanquam rex cœlestis cum summo honore, in
♑. *pusillanimis*, in ♒. *pauperrimus presbyter*, in ♓. *& potens magni
honoris ac divitiarum*, in ♈. *dux fortunatissimus in bello*, in ♉. *amore
captus*, in ♊. *mercator bonæ fidei*, in ♋. *principum amicus & in pretio
apud magnates*, in ♌. *sapiens & amabilis*, in ♍. *scientia præditus*, in
♎. *Episcopus, aut dives in rebus Ecclesiæ*, in ♏. *amicus alicujus
principis*. Sic porro, si ea pars Zodiaci, quæ *Arieti* attribuitur, oriatur, in
qua *Mars* cognoscitur suum habere dominium, ipse in ea describetur
curru vectus, ensemque manu tenens, & fulgura ab oculis ejiciens, in ♉.
rapiens violenter fœminam sub forma militis communis, in ♊. *animam
Ulyssis simulans*, in ♋. *inconstans & temerarius*, in ♌. *seipsum
interficiens aut suspendens*, in ♍. *fingens literas aut Sagittas ab arcu
mittens*, in ♎. *cum Venere in adulterio deprehensus a Vulcano*, in ♏.
dives in possessionibus, in ♐. *conductor exercitus*, in ♑. *alios gladio
vulnerans*, in ♒. *audax & magna aggrediens*, in ♓. *amicus Regis*. Tum
postea, si Leo oriatur, & se supra horizontem, cum suo Domino, videlicet
Sole, commonstraverit, *Apollo* in eo dignitatem Imperatoris habebit, &
in ♍. *justitiam exercebit*, in ♎. *mercator erit res ponderans*; in ♏. *cum
serpente Pythone pugnabit*, in ♐. *sagittas suas huc atque illuc
ejaculabitur*, in ♑. *tristis erit & obscurus*, in ♒. *per flumen navigare
videbitur*, in ♓. *cum Oceano ei res erit*, in ♈. *erit biliosus atque
iracundus*, in ♉. *cum Minotauro belligerabitur*; in ♊. *cum Castore &
Polluce familiaritatem habebit*, & sic in cæteris: *Taurus* enim surgens,
Venerem in sua domo habebit, ipsaque more *Europæ* insidebit dorso
tauri: Sic in ascendentibus *Geminis*, imaginabimur *Mercurium*: atque
itidem quoque ascendente *Cancro*, *Lunam*, procedendo cum illis
successive & gradatim, uti fecimus cum superioribus.

CAP. V.
De imaginibus minus principalibus.

Aliquibus fortasse minus placebit umbrarum minus principalium multitudo. Ut itaque iis gratiosior sit hæc ars exclusis imaginibus, sciendum est, locos illos posse coloribus ab invicem distingui hoc modo: *Primus locus* erit albus instar prati nive cooperti, *Secundus* sit rubicundus, habeatque effigiem prati existentis ante portam theatri, in quo prælium fuit commissum, ita ut ejus superficies sanguine tincta colorem rubicundum exhibeat, *Tertius* locus sit viridis & area quædam ante portam gramine arboribusque virentibus conspicua, *Quartus* sit cæruleus, & undequaque instar vallis ante portam fontibus irriguus; *Quintus* & ultimus sit specus seu spelunca subterranea obscurissima, nigrum præ se ferens colorem. His pratis oppositæ fingantur *quinque columnæ*, quæ itidem debent figura & colore distingui; *Figura* enim *duarum extremarum erit circularis & rotunda, media* autem columna *habebit figuram hexagoneam*, & quæ his *intermedia* sunt *quadratam*

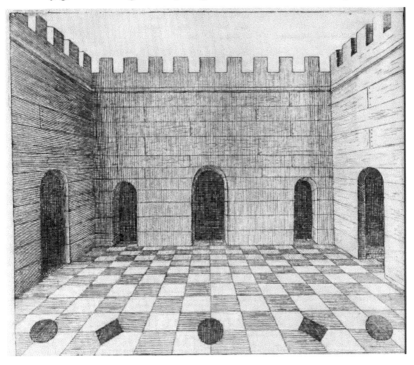

Sequitur figura vera theatri

117

possidebunt figuram: Colore etiam hoc modo ab invicem different, ut colores earum relationem habeant cum coloribus portarum theatri iis oppositarum, opposita tamen seu inversa ratione: ita scilicet ut albedo nigredini obiiciatur, &c. Poteris etiam hisce columnis annulos phantastico conceptu & catenas affigere, quibus adligata animalia significabunt *Adverbia, Conjunctiones, Praepositiones & Interjectiones*, uti in sententiis dicetur. Eritque in illis hic ordo: *Albae columnae* fingatur affixus annulus argenteus, cum tali quoque catena, *Rubrae* vero cupreus cum catena ex ramo facta; & *Lividae* plumbeus cum catena plumbea, ac *Nigrae* denique ferreus annulus cum ferrea itidem catena affixus existimetur. Ubi autem vocabula sunt significativa, ibi necesse est, ut illa denotentur per imaginem aut idaeam magis principalem, & non aliter, ut in sententiarum recordatione apparebit.

CAP. VI.
Quot modis imagines magis principales possint in locis vacuis exprimi, tam in arte rotunda, quam quadrata.

Actiones, quibus imagines in locis exprimuntur, *solent esse* aut	*Crudeles*, videlicet cum aliquis videt rem quandam immanem, aut facinus quoddam crudeliter, & contra naturae leges patrari: cujus generis sunt, *Tyrannus aliquem interimens, Lucretia seipsam e medio tollens.*
	Ridiculosae, veluti, si *foemina ex asino decidens denudet sua secretiora*, & omnes aliae res dignae risu.
	Miraculosae, veluti *si occurrat homo duobus capitibus natus*, vel *asinus doceat aliquem canere fidibus aut ipsemet etiam doctus evadat.*
	Obscaenae & turpes: ut *si quis in re inhonesta versetur, eaque turpiter afficiatur.*

Et hujusmodi etiam actionibus uti possunt imagines aut ideae coelestes, quas imaginari possumus in pratis illis antea descriptis. Hic autem notare debemus, quod unumquodque theatrum tibi dabit quinque portas videlicet, *Albam, Rubram, Viridem, Cœruleam & Nigram.* Hic etiam velim te inprimis observare, quod plurimum huic arti conferat, si in sphæra Zodiaci sive stellata imagineris historias loco & actione cuique signo & ejus loco convenientes: verbi gratia; *ad signum Arietis pertinet historia aurei Velleris Jasonis & Medeæ: Prima igitur idea* ante portam albam erit Medeæ in summitate montis Atlantis, herbas suas magicas colligentis nive coopertas; *Secunda* ante portam rubram erit Medea fratrem suum interficiens membraque ejus in prati herbas projiciens: *Tertia* erit Medea herbas colligens in tempe Thessaliæ, virgultis, arboribusque viridibus vigente, ut Jasonis conamini queat assistere. *Quarta* erit Jason & Medea navem ingrediens cum vellere aureo. *Quinta* erit domus aut locus ille obscurus, in quo tauri & draco, aurei velleris custodes, incantatione ligati & inclusi manserunt, & sic in cæteris.

CAP. VII.

Quot modis utraque arte, videlicet tam in rotunda, quam in quadrata exprimantur vocabula significativa?

Expressio vocabuli significativi fit *tribus modis*, scilicet	*Relatione,* scilicet, cum res aliqua alteri refertur, ita ut per eam relationem, significet rem aliquam sine rei significandæ expressione: Sic *atramentum potest significare atramentarium, nigredo atramentum, vagina gladium.*
	Similitudine: nempe cum res similis in loco expressa indicat eam cui similis est, veluti *Sirenes fœminas, Henricus pauper coronatus, Henricum Regem Galliæ,* &c.
	Reali[56] *præsentia:* sic *imago aut idea gladio aliquem percutiens significabit gladium.* Hæc igitur est, cum res vera in sua natura & substantia in loco aliquo ab imaginis vel ideæ actione exprimitur.

De animæ memorativæ scientia.

CAP. I.
Quotuplex sit vocabulum: Et de modo explicandi in locis vocabula significativa.

Vocabulum significativum appello illud, quod per vivam aliquam imaginis, aut ideæ actionem in loco aliquo explicari potest: *Non significativum* vero, quod in locis per se propter actionis defectum significari non potest.

	Significativa, ut sunt	*Verba*, ut interficere, saltare, canere, &c.			
		Substantiva, ut, liber, ensis, taurus, &c.			
		Adjectiva, ut, fortis, violentus, tristis, hilaris, &c.			
		Participia, ut percutiens, ardens, ægrotans, &c.			
Vocabula omnia sunt aut			*Minus significativa*, ut	*Adverbia*, ut, non, nunc.	
				Conjunctiones, ut, &, nec, atque.	
				Præpositiones, ut, per, in.	
				Interjectiones, ut, proh, vah.	
		Audita			*Propria*, ut, Petrus, Johannes, Sara, Maria, &c.
				Substantiva nomina	
	Non significativa		*Magis significativa*, ut		*Non propria*, ut, labor, intellectus, spiritus, &c.
				Pronomina, ut, qui, ille, iste, meus, &c.	
		Inaudita, ut, Gorocoga, Abricalac, Arbroc, &c.			

CAP. II.
De vocabulorum significativorum recordatione in arte sphærica.

Locis, ut supra dictum est, distinctis & descripta in primo theatro historia Medeæ per quinque prata, oportet per regulam prædictam in vocabulorum significativorum expressione operari hoc modo, videlicet si vocabulum (*Liber*) velim in primo loco denotare, imaginabor Medeam in prato albo, tanquam subtilem spiritum in æthere pendentem aut in curru igneo sedentem, inspicere librum magicum: Atque hæc talis imaginatio debet reali expressione in loco sibi proprio notari. Porro secundum vocabulum sit (*exaltabat*) possumus igitur fingere, spiritum istum Medeæ in turris summitate prospicere & anxie observare, an Pater eam persequatur, nec ne. *Tertium* vocabulum sit (*Lætus*) quod ut explicetur imaginabimur, spiritum Medeæ lætari duplici nomine, tum scilicet propter loci amœnitatem, tum etiam, quod invenit herbas proposito suo inservientes. *Quartum* vocabulum sit (*cultellus*) Medeam igitur cultellum suum, quo fratrem jugulavit, in mare projicere nobis persuadeamus. *Quintum* vocabulum sit (*Lux*). Quod ut significetur, imaginabimur, quod in conflictu Jasonis cum serpente vigilante & tauris flammas evomentibus eximia lux & ingens scintillarum multitudo ex spelunca prosiliat. Et sic progrediendum ad theatrum ♈. occidentale, in cujus obscuritate essentiales Medeæ actiones, tanquam reflectentes umbras speculari debemus.

CAP. III.
De vocabulorum significativorum recordatione & positione in arte quadrata.

Si vocabula fuerint significativa, exprimentur aut *relatione*, aut *similitudine*, aut *reali præsentia*: Sic vocabuli (*Leo*) significationem exprimam in prima primi loci porta per relationem, videlicet per Sampsonem leonina pelle amictum, aut reali actione per Sampsonem cum leone pugnantem: si secundum vocabulum sit (*Ensis*) imaginabimur per relationem, quod Dalila iracundiæ ardore percita rumpat inventam mariti vaginam, aut etiam reali actione fingemus, quod desperata mortem sibi gladio consciscat. Quod si tertium vocabulum sit (*musca*) fingemus, aut reali præsentia, quod aliquis Philistæorum studens evitare Sampsonis violentiam & fervorem, insideat muscæ & evolet in aërem; aut relatione quod carnes habeat putridas a muscis undique corruptas, aut similitudine, quod alis, muscæ simillimis fugiat ex loco uno in alium.

CAP. IV.

De vocabulorum cognitorum quidem, sed aut omnino non,
aut difficulter significativorum in utraque arte recordatione.

In *arte rotunda* solent *nomina substantiva, adjectiva & participia* per ordinem alphabeticum Deorum, cum aliqua tamen eorum circa fixam imaginem actione explicari. Sic Neptunus nihil faciens vel otiosus significabit, nihil. *Verba non significativa* exprimuntur per alphabetum Dearum, ut Proserpina in magna majestate significat posse: *Pronomina* porro omnia indicant ut aut vitio aliquo, quod erit monstrum vel Diabolus, aut virtute, quæ erit Angelus: sic (*ille*) explicabitur per monstrum aliquod leprosum, & maculis repletum, digito aliquid ostendens. *Adverbia* autem *Conjunctiones, Præpositiones & Interjectiones*, solent per bruta cœlestia significari. Atque sic etiam sese res habet in *arte quadrata*, hoc solo excepto, quod pro vitiis & virtutibus aves solent usurpari: sint tamen hæc omnia cum notabili aliqua actione conjuncta aut indicata: Possumus etiam totum animal aliquando per notabilem & distinctam quandam ejus partem denotare, ut *Leonem* per caudam, pellem vel ungues, *Elephantem* per dentes aut nasum retortum, *Pantheram* per relationem inter illum & rem aliquam maculis infectam, atque etiam per pellem, *Asinum* per lyram, *Bovem* per cornua, *Hydram* per venenum, *Camelum* per vestimenta Sancti Johannis, *Gryphum* per alam cum cauda leonis, *Quæstorem* per linguam aut canem, *Rhinocerotem* per cornu, *Simiam* per imitationem, aut hominem simiæ similem, *Ursam* per plaustrum cœleste, *Felem* per murem aut ignem, *Mulum* per onera, *Equum* per frænum, *Agnum* per lanam, *Adamum* per pomum, *Bonifacium Papam* per clavem, *Cadmum* per serpentem aut arborem, *Davidem* per Goliæ caput, *Eteoclem* per flammam divisam, *sanctum Franciscum* per crucem sanguineam, *Herculem* per fustem aut arcum, *Jasonem* per vellus aureum aut infidelitatem, *Midam* per aurum, aut aures asininas aureas, *Nestorem* per barbam albam, *Orpheum* per lyram, *Prometheum* per cor sanguineum aut vulturem, *Quintilianum* per Grammaticam aut virgam, *Raimundum Lullium* per phialam & alembicum, *Sinonem* per equum ligneum, *Tantalum* per famem aut pomum in aqua, *Ulyssem* per Syrenes, &c. Sic ponitur pro *Aquila* oculus aspiciens Solem, pro *Bubone* obscuritas, pro *Corvo* nigredo, pro *Drepane* hyrundo, pro *Erithaco* homo solus in desertis, pro *Falcone* tintinnabulum, pro *Grue* locus aquaticus, rostrum acutum, vel herba geranium, pro *Hyrundine* tectum domus, pro *Ibe* parvulus serpens. Atque ita semper sese res habebit in distinctione formarum conceptarum in arte rotunda respiciendo assidue ad prædictas exceptiones.

CAP. V.
De nominum propriorum cognitorum recordatione.

Cum nomina propria cognita atque communia vis recordari, oportet te alios eorundem nominum, qui vel familiariter, vel ex historiarum lectione tibi cogniti sunt, in locis collocare, & quidem simpliciter actione tali, quali communiter uti consueverunt: Verbi gratia, si meminisse voluero alicujus *Caroli*, collocabo ibi quendam Carolum bene mihi cognitum: qui quidem, si Notarius, Secretarius, aut faber ferrarius fuerit, &c. ille quoque hoc officio in loco illo, ubi ponendus venit, cum evidenti imaginis adjumento, & notabili ejusdem actione fungetur, vel etiam eligam quendam in historiis clarum, veluti Carolum Magnum belligerantem contra infideles. Sic si *Clementis* velim recordari, ponam in loco meo communi, Papam Clementem cum cornu in manu pro meliore distinctione, & sic in cæteris.

CAP. VI.
De nominum propriorum, nunquam tibi ante auditorum, recordatione.

In hac regula maxime requiruntur *ordines alphabetici*: Nam bestia *primam* significabit literam, homo, *secundam*, res mortua *tertiam*, & avis *quartam*, idque non sine eximia imaginis actione, quæ rem aliquam non decentem peraget cum bruto, homine & ave; Exempli gratia, Angeli, teste Sibylla, qui custodes sunt, numerantur *Heromiel, Saniel, Uriel*, &c. In loco primo igitur pono Hydram, quæ veneno suo interficit principalem loci imaginem, & super dorso Hydræ imaginabor Eteoclem ardentem, tenentem manu labrum, ut aqua ejus ignem extinguat, sed olor instans ejus capiti omnem aquam magna siti percitus, ebibit, quare hic non restat, nisi *miel*, quod facillimum est recordari, retento *Hero*; Nam *Hydra* significat H. *Eteocles* E. *Labrum* R. & *Olor* O. Actio autem erit, ut tangens hydram concidat mortuus. *Secundo loco* ponam Simiam, quam Adam ex Paradiso ducens furca sæpissime percutiat: Sanguinem autem a simia dimanantem fingam nutrire Ibem avem: Actio itaque imaginis essentialis erit, ut Adamum vulneret, quia sæpissime in domum suam introivit cum Simia & Ibe sua. *Tertio loco* collocabo Ursam in cujus dorsum elevabitur Raimundus Lullius cum phialis & alembicis. Ursa autem furibunda rumpet seu confringet phialas, eaque propter a Raimundo percutietur pistillo. Sed & alio quodam modo faciliori, hoc idem poterit fieri: Etenim si in continenti volueris aliquod vocabulum antea tibi inauditum memoria retinere, pones in locis destinatis alia quædam vocabula, aut propria nomina, aut alias significativa, quæ exprimant omnes fere aut aliquot syllabas illius tui vocabuli inauditi, cujus recordari cupis; Verbi gratia: Si velis recordari Uriel ponetur primo loco Urias, qui jussu Davidis fuit in bello interfectus, & quia hæc dictio exprimit duas syllabas nominis tui inauditi aut inusitati, idcirco imaginaberis eum fuisse furca interfectum, quæ significat duo: Constitues autem illum in dextra loci tui parte, ut admonearis, eum denotare primas syllabas, et in sinistra parte collocabis Eliam ascendentem in cœlum, ac tenentem manu lanceam, quæ significabit syllabam unam, & sic in cæteris. Hoc modo etiam poteris in arte rotunda operari.

CAP. VII.
De sententiarum recordatione tam in arte rotunda, quam in quadrata.

Posteaquam perfectum vocabulorum significativorum modum didicisti, poteris, si ad amussim volueris operari, collocare omnia vocabula ordine convenienti in singulari aliquo loco, ut ita inter se distincta habeantur: sed quia illud in multitudine sententiarum tædiosum foret & infinitum, idcirco alia incedemus via: Observentur igitur in hoc opere sequentes regulæ *primo* scilicet ut perfectum alicujus membri sensum exprimas vera aliqua & propria actione; verbi gratia, in hac sententia, *Corporum prima divisio est in simplicia*, finges, quod imago quædam dividat corpora, aut divisionem faciat in elementa, quæ sunt simplicia; *secundo* si vocabulum incipiens aut initiale sit non significativum, aut difficulter significari possit, tunc exprimes illud per imaginem, ut in secundo libro dictum est; ita faciet illud actionem cum vocabulo proxime sequenti: veluti, *omnis motus simplex aut rectus est aut rotundus*: Hic Orpheus movebitur recte & rotunde; aut Sol formabitur in manu, significans motum per relationem. *Tertio* si duo vel tria adverbia aut conjunctiones, &c. inchœnt sententiam oportet illa in uno tantum loco exprimere, ni consequentia sint manifesta, et in sensus natura inseparabilia. *Quarto*, cum exacte volueris & subito dictas membri particulas in locos suos disponere, assignabis prius imaginibus actiones fictorum vocabulorum significativorum: Ut, si collocavero atramentum in primo loco, & primum membrum fuerit illud: *Forma dat nomen & esse rei*; fingam, imaginem tollere atramentum, & post abstersionem ejus de facie cujusdam formosæ puellæ, appellare illam Mauram. Cum autem volueris hæc peragere in arte rotunda oportebit uti 10. portis Medeæ, & deinde Europæ, &c.

CAP. VIII.
De orationibus & carminibus.

In orationibus & Carminibus opus prædicta propositione & eodem præcise modo; sed & in Carminibus facillime id præstatur propter mensuræ necessitatem.

CAP. IX.
De subjectis & quotupliciter subjectum hic accipiatur.

Subjectum, uti hoc loco illud accipitur, *est actio perfecta alicujus intentionis, quæ vel relatione aliqua, vel similitudine vel saltem realiter in uno solum loco exprimitur: Actionem* autem *perfectam* alicujus intentionis voco illam, qua sensus alicujus historiæ vel dicti sapientis, vel legis, vel aphorismi aut consimilium exprimitur, & perfecte in loco aliquo explicatur: sed quia in his omnibus varius est operandi modus, idcirco ordine quodam & methodice progrediemur. In historiarum igitur subjectis sciendum est, quod *historia duplici modo in locis exprimatur*, videlicet, *aut generaliter aut specialiter. Generaliter* exprimitur historia cum tota ejus series & sensus in unico solummodo loco explicatur, ut si generaliter velim totam secundi libri Æneidos historiam Virgilianam in loco aliquo exprimere, fingam, quod imago loci in summitate montis eminus conspiciat, qua ratione ingens equus ligneus de nocte in urbem introducatur, adeoque etiam deinceps, cæca adhuc nocte, ipsa urbs lamentabili modo omni ex parte accendatur. *Specialiter* autem historia exprimitur, cum unaquæque ejus pars seorsim explicatur.

CAP. X.
De modo exprimendi figuras arithmeticas in prædictis locis.

Hujus rei mentionem fecimus in libro nostro *de Arithmetica universali*, ubi etiam particulariter de Arithmetica memoriali caput unum atque alterum proposuimus, eaque ratione docuimus modum numerandi, addendi, subtrahendi, multiplicandi & dividendi per aptam figurarum memorialium positionem, in locis convenientibus. Quocirca vos ad illum tractatum nostrum hinc remittimus, ut breviter huic sectionis secundæ portioni finem imponemus.

[FINIS]

Fludd on "Mathematical Memory"

(Extract 1: Book X of *De Arithmetico Universali*)

LIBER DECIMUS
De Arithmetica Memoriali.

CAP. I.
De locis memorialibus.

Regula I.

In Arithmetica memoriali locorum memorialium situs est semper observandus; ita tamen, ut loci ultimi quadrati pars inferior conjungatur in sua continuitate cum loco primo ex parte dextra, & loco quarto ex parte sinistra, ita, ut ex tribus locis unus tantum fiat, ut in exemplo sequenti apparet.

3		2
4	5	Locus 1

Descriptio locorum quadrati secundum
artem memoriæ simplicem.

3	2	Prima series.
Locus pro aggregato numero Additioni, Subtractioni & Multiplicationi aptus.		

Regula II.

Prædicta etiam loca seriem duorum numerorum facillime per conceptum retinebunt, si duplex in quolibet loco fiat actio, nempe ab ejus parte inferiore ad partem superiorem, hoc modo. Fingatur, *in primo loco* hominem vel puellam collocari, poma vel nuces, vel aliquem alium fructum, ut ab arbore decidat, expectantem. *In secundo* vero loco fiat conceptus, ut aliqui campanas in summitate turris altissimæ pendentes pulsare videantur. *In tertio* lupum vel vulpem homines in patibulo pendentes pulsare videantur. *In tertio* lupum vel vulpem homines in patibulo pendentes avide intueri. *Putabis eo modo, ut in figura proxime sequenti 1.*

Regula III.

Si plures fuerint in additione, subtractione vel multiplicatione series super tectum hujus quadrati, oportet adjungere tria loca alterius quadrati, ea etiam duplici impressione implendo. In illius enim *prima parte* pontem mente tua describas; super quem stabit piscator quidam, qui piscem satis magnum hamo e flumine extrahere videbitur. Similiter, *si plura loca in his speciebus requirantur, necesse erit loca unius quadrati illis alterius collateraliter connectere, simpliciter aut dupliciter, prout addendorum series fuerint in numero,* ut in figura sequenti 2.

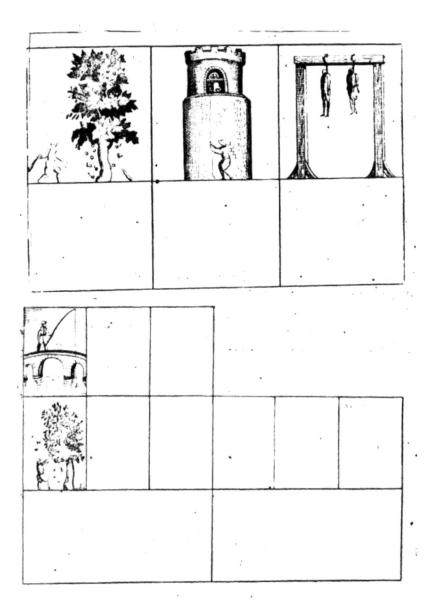

CAP. II.
De additione.

Regula I.

Sint ergo numeri addendi 164. 335. Concipiat imaginatio, hominem pileo quadrato coopertum, avide fructum arboris appetentem cornu suum violenter projecisse contra fructus, illudque vi istius ictus in frusta minuta confregisse, cujus partes ruptæ pileum ipsius dilacerabunt. In secundo loco fingatur, limacem cornibus suis hominem campanam pulsantem vulnerasse, quo viso campana tripodem super ipsum deorsum deturbans limacem interfecit. In tertio loco imprimatur in intellectu, lupum hasta, & aliis modis tentare capistrum hominis suspensi discindere, quæ dum est facturus, tripes patibulum cadendo deterruit illum, & fugavit.

Regula II.

Adduntur autem prædictæ figuræ conversione duarum figurarum in tertiam. Nam pileus, & cornu primi ordinis transmutantur in serpentem, limax & tripes in caudam canis, cum qua propter actionis vivacitatem serpens belligerabit. Similiter sub tertia serie locorum tertia metamorphosis, seu transmutatio hastæ & patibuli in librum quadratum erit expressa, ut infra.

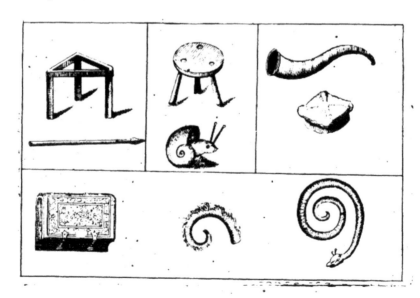

CAP. III.
De subtractione.

Regula I.
Iisdem mediis subtractio in hac arte fit, nempe locorum bases a serie superiori subtrahendo, & transformatum in loco fundamentali collocando. Sic character 4. nempe *pileus*, subtractus a charactere 5. *cornu* scilicet, generat characterem 1. *hastam*, & sic in cæteris, ut in Arithmetica vulgari habetur.

CAP. IV.
De Multiplicatione.

In multiplicatione, ubi multiplicator est articulus, eadem plane est ratio. Sed quia aliquando multiplicator ex multis conflatur articulis, ideo locus fundamentalis in 3. vel plures dividitur partes æquales secundum ejus longitudinem, quarum una erit viridis, altera alba, & tertia rubicunda. Hisce enim distinctionibus multiplicanda melius & dilucidius explicari possunt, & hoc etiam sequenti exemplo explicatur. Quod autem aggregatum fuerit in multiplicatione, in parte nigra debet exprimi.

Multi-	plicand-	da
Multi-	plican -	tia
Viridis locus		
Locus albus		
Rubicundus		
Locus niger		

CAP. V.
De partitione.

Quia rarissime in hac arte ultima hac Arithmeticæ specie uti solent, tum ob difficultatem prompti ejusdem conceptus, tum propter multitudines operationum ejus, quibus confusio in Artistæ imaginatione gigneretur, nullam de ea hoc loco mentionem faciemus; sed eam acutioribus aliorum indagationibus inveniendam relinquemus, gradus nostros ad Arithmeticam jocosam accelerando, qua conceptum nostrum, vanis jamdudum imaginationibus defessum, aliquantisper tandem reficiemus.

(Extract 2: Book I Chapter X of *De Arithmetico Universali*)

CAP. X.
De numeris memorialibus

Numeri sive *figuræ memoriales* sunt vel	*Digiti*, quorum unus est	Unitatis, ut	Hasta / Pistillum	
		Binarius, ut	Furca / Forfex	
		Ternarius, ut	Tripes / Patibulum triangulare	
		Quaternarius, ut	Liber / Pileus quadratus	
		Quinarius, ut	Cucumis / Lituus	
		Senarius, ut	Limax / Retorta	
		Septenarius, ut	Securis / Quadratum Geometricum	
		Octonarius, ut	Perspicillum / Nates	
		Novenarius	Serpens circumvolutus / Cauda canis	
	Articuli, qui sic exprimuntur	Asinus hasta percussus	denotabit {	10
		Asinus forficibus tonsus		20
		Asinus super tripodem sedens		30
		Asinus librum legens		40
		Homo duos asinos hasta percutiens		100
	Compositi ex	*Digitis* tantum, ut si	Homo pharmacopolam manibus pistillum tenentem hasta percusserit, actio talis significabit 11 / Homo vel Pharmacopola forfices tonsoris pistillo comminuat 12 / Petrus hasta Johannem super tripodem sedentem interfecerit, hæc actio significabit 13 / Tonsor pileum quadratum alicui eripuerit, & forficibus consciderit serpentem, ipsum mordicantem significabit 249	
		Articulis & digitis simul, ut quidam posuit librum sub securi, ut eam destruat; Asinus vero librum conservandi gratia eripiens graviter vulneratur, & ista actio significabit, 470.		

NUMERORUM DESCRIPTIO

Asinus significabit ciphram, quia (ut dicunt) Asinus nihil valet.

11	Undecim significatur pistillo hasta, aut duobus pistillis, aut duplici hasta: debitisque actionibus significari debet.
9136	Hic numerus, angue præcedenti & homine hasta eum persequenti, & in persequutione sua per patibulum transeunti & limacem super illud scandentem hasta sua interficiente in memoria præfiguratur.
2000	Hujusmodi etiam numerus intentionaliter exprimitur, conceptione trium asinorum hominem furcam gerentem oribus apertis persequentium, & minantium: Atque sic in omnibus reliquis figuris agendum erit..

Regula I.

Pro unoquoque digito duas descripsimus figuras varietatis causa; quia duo numeri ejusdem speciei sæpe concurrunt, qui, si eadem figura in locis memorialibus simul conjunctis exprimerentur, memoriam procul dubio perturbarent; Diversitate enim reficitur memoria; Sic 224. vel 111. non sunt duabus furcis, vel tribus hastis exprimenda; quia plurima similia species impressas confundent.

Regula II.

Numeri memoriales viva semper actione in locis debitis demonstrari debent; quo diutius & firmius in mente retineantur.

Regula III.

Numerus memorialis per relationem aliquando est exprimendus; *ut* si binarius numerus sit designandus, imaginabimur tonsorem per se absque forficibus ibi collocatum esse, cum actione conveniente; si vero unitas, militem, si numerus ternarius, carnificem; Tonsor enim forficibus, Miles hasta, & Carnifex patibulo referetur.

Regula IV.

Verus figurarum ordo actionum sequetur seriem. Actor enim principalis primum possidebit locum, a sinistra numerando; Deinde qui ejus actionem immediate patietur, erit secundus actor, secundumque sibi locum vendicabit, & ita in sequentibus; Ut si 48. retinenda veniant, sit quidam Doctor pileo quadrato indutus; pileus autem cadens percutiat perspicillum ejus, in locum secundum, quod casu suo confringatur.

FOOTNOTES TO MAIN TEXT

1   This may or may not be a reference to the pineal gland or 'third eye'. Fludd's near-contemporary René Descartes was known to have a keen interest in this structure, but those of his works that mention it (*Les Passions de l'âme* of 1649 and *L'Homme*, written before 1637 but only published more than a decade after his death in 1650) post-date the present volume. For a possible relationship between this illustration and the Vault of Christian Rosenkreutz, see Rafał Prinke, *The Great Work in the Theatre of the World* in *A Compendium on the Rosicrucian Vault,* ed. Adam McLean, Edinburgh 1985.

2   For their possible identities, see Luca Guariento, *Life, Friends and Associations of Robert Fludd: A Revised Account,* JEMS 5 (2016), 1:9-37, page 17, footnote 49. https://www.academia.edu/38279617/Life_Friends_and_Associations_o f_Robert_Fludd_A_Revised_Account

3   Charles de Lorraine, 4th Duke of Guise (2 August 1571 – 30 September 1640) was the son of Henry I, Duke of Guise and Catherine of Cleves.

4   Presumably Claude de Lorraine (5 June 1578 – 24 January 1657), also called Claude de Guise, husband of Marie de Rohan.

5   Fludd has *hunc Mitilenæ militem*, 'this soldier of Mytilene', i.e. a soldier from the capital of Lesbos, but it is hard to know what he could mean by that. J. B. Craven, in his *Dr. Robert Fludd* (1902), p. 85, refers to the Duke's brother as 'a knight of Malta' (which in Latin would be *Melitæ eques*). An alternative possibility is that Fludd had *three* students in Marseilles: the Duke, his brother, and an unidentified Greek soldier, which would explain Fludd's unusual phraseology: 'this soldier'.

6   Lat. *penetralia*, a word with strong religious overtones. This whole passage suggests that, even at this stage, Fludd may already have been engaging esoterically with the Art of Memory.

7   Almost certainly the choroid plexus. See Introduction, section III.

8   *myrothecium*. Holyoke's *Large Dictionary* of 1677 translates this as 'a box of sweet ointments'. Cicero uses the word in his *Ad Atticum* 2.1.1. to describe the box of rhetorical tricks he has learned from Isocrates. In religious literature it is sometimes used of the virtues of the Virgin Mary. The German translator in Volume 2 of *Documenta Mnemonica* renders it as *Wachstafel*, 'wax tablet'; see *Documenta Mnemonica, Das enzyklopädische Gedächtnis der Frühen Neuzeit,* ed. Berns and Neuber, Max Niemeyer Verlag, Tübingen 1998, vol. II, pp. 78-131.

9   Latin *dilatatio*, which in Late Latin usually means *extension* (i.e. a horizontal movement), but which can also mean *swelling or expansion*

(i.e. a vertical movement). In religious texts, e.g. those of Richard of St. Victor, it can also signify a higher state of spiritual expansion. See the Introduction, section III.

10   This section echoes a passage in the opening pages of *The Golden Ass* of Apuleius: "Nevertheless, lately at Athens, before the Painted Porch, I beheld with both my eyes a conjurer, who swallowed a two-handed horseman's sword that had a very sharp edge, and afterwards, for a small sum of money, buried in his lowest viscera a hunting spear so as to have that part of it downward which threatens destruction. And lo! the iron head of the spear having passed through the groin, and being forced out again through the hinder part of the head, an effeminately beautiful boy was seen dancing on the other extremity of the spear. This boy, in dancing, turned and twisted himself as if he had been without nerves and bones, to the admiration of all that were present; so that you would have said it was the noble serpent, which adheres with slippery embraces to the half-amputated branches of the knotted staff of the medical god" (Thomas Taylor's translation, slightly adapted). But who 'Peter' is, we have no idea.

11   The Ring of Solomon or Solomon's Seal is the signet ring attributed to King Solomon in medieval Jewish tradition and in Islamic and Western occultism. It was often depicted as either a pentagram or hexagram (in which case Jewish tradition refers to it as the Star of David). It gave Solomon the power to command demons, genies or talk to animals. The Wand of Solomon (*virgula*) referred to in footnote *xi* is presumably the one referred to and illustrated in the early Italian Renaissance grimoire known as the *Clavicula Salomonis*. It should not be confused with the larger and heavier Staff of Solomon (*baculus*), which bears the same inscription. Our illustration is taken from Plate XIII of S. L. MacGregor Mathers' translation from Hebrew based on Add. MSS., 10,862; Sloane MSS., 1307 and 3091; Harleian MSS., 3981; King's MSS., 288; and Lansdowne MSS., 1202 and 1203. The *Clavicula* says that "the Staff should be of elderwood, or cane, or rosewood; and the Wand of hazel or nut tree, in all cases the wood being virgin, that is of one year's growth only. They should each be cut from the tree at a single stroke, on the day of Mercury, at sunrise. The characters shown should be written or engraved thereon in the day and hour of Mercury." See *The Key of Solomon the King (Clavicula Salomonis). Trans. and ed. S. Liddell MacGregor Mathers* [1889]. Foreword by R. A. Gilbert. Boston/York Beach, ME: Weiser Books, 2000, p. 116. Frances Yates suggests that the 'someone in Toulouse' may have been Jean Belot, 'curé de Milmonts', the author of *Instruction familière et très-facile pour apprendre les sciences de chiromance et physiognomie* (1619). Belot was a palmist who used the human hand as the memory palace, an idea we find

anticipated in *De Arte Reminiscentiæ, per loca, et imagines, ac per notas et figuras in manibus positas* (1602) by the Franciscan friar Girolamo Marafioti. We hope to publish transcriptions and English translations of the works by Belot and Marafioti in due course.

12　This illustration is our own interpolation: it does not appear in the original text.

13　We have retained the usual Ciceronian term locus to indicate the container or receptacle for the memory-image, as Frances Yates explains: "The artificial memory is established from places and images (*Constat igitur artificiosa memoria ex locis et imaginibus*), the stock definition to be forever repeated down the ages. A *locus* is a place easily grasped by the memory, such as a house, an intercolumnar space, a corner, an arch, or the like. Images are forms, marks or simulacra (*formæ, notæ, simulacra*) of what we wish to remember. For instance if we wish to recall the genus of a horse, of a lion, of an eagle, we must place their images on definite *loci*" (*The Art of Memory*, Routledge reprint 1999, p. 6).

14　Lat. *loci communes*. This seems to be Fludd's own term for the subdivisions of the memory-palace to which the *loci* are assigned.

15　From William of Ockham, *Summa Totius Logicæ*, i. 12. A variant of the famous 'Ockham's Razor'.

16　Fludd has *quinque*, five, which is presumably an error for *quindecim*.

17　This phrase has caused some controversy. See Frances Yates, *Giordano Bruno and the Art of Memory*, p. 332: "On the bay window of the 'theatre' are inscribed the words THEATRUM ORBI. Since Fludd and the highly educated engraver certainly knew Latin it seems difficult to believe that this can be a mistake for THEATRUM ORBIS [i.e. Theatre of the World]. I suggest therefore (though with diffidence) that the dative case is intentional and that the inscription means, not that this is a 'Theatre of the World' but one of the 'theatres' or stages to be placed with or in the world, that is in the heavens shown on the opposite page." There may however be a clue in the opening passage of the *Oration on the Dignity of Man* by Pico della Mirandola: "I have read in the writings of the Arabs that Abdullah the Saracen, when asked what seemed to him most marvellous in this *theatre of the world* replied that nothing seemed to him more splendid than man. And this accords with the famous saying of Mercurius Trismegistus, 'What a miracle is man, O Asclepius'." (my emphasis). Now the term Pico uses for 'theatre of the world' is not *teatrum orbi* but *mundana scaena*, but the underlying idea seems to be a very similar one. Perhaps this was the source for Fludd's term. Note the circles, squares and hexagon on the floor.

18　The classically-educated Fludd naturally used Greek and Roman myth and legend as his thesaurus of 'stories'. The modern Memory Artist is of course at liberty to use whatever material they might find suitable and convenient.

19   We are giving Fludd's Latin sequences here with English translations. The Memory Artist can either use these or make up similar lists in English (or indeed any other language) while adhering to Fludd's rules.

20   This word is a puzzle, as it seems to be unknown to Latin lexicography. The insect known as the *castor bean tick* (*I. ricinus*) is sometimes mistakenly called *Iricinus*, and we have assumed that this is what Fludd means here. The German translation in Volume 2 of *Documenta Mnemonica* assumes it is a mistake for *Ericius*, 'hedgehog', but it cannot be that, as the word must begin with an I to be in sequence.

21   In Greek mythology, Nereus was the father of the fifty sea nymphs known as the Nereids. Attic vase-painters often depicted him as a man from the waist up and a fish from the waist down, i.e. a merman.

22   Another lexicographical mystery. The Germans in their *Documenta Mnemonica* translate it as *coyote*. Later in the text Fludd identifies it simply as 'an animal that barks like a dog', but he does not make it clear whether he means any barking animal, or one specific kind. Semantically, a *questor* (not *quæstor* as Fludd spells it) would be an animal that howls or wails.

23   Blue seems to be an emblematic colour for hope, certainly in English inn-signs.

24   Once again we have left the names in Latin. Memory Artists can either use these or invent their own, e.g. Adam, Bernard, Charles, David, Edward, Francis, etc.

25   In Greek mythology Ixion was king of the Lapiths, the most ancient tribe of Thessaly. After trying to seduce Hera he was expelled from Olympus and blasted with a thunderbolt. Zeus also ordered Hermes to bind Ixion to a winged fiery wheel that was always spinning (in early versions of the story through the heavens, but in later myth in Tartarus). Only when Orpheus played his lyre during his trip to the Underworld to rescue Eurydice did the spinning temporarily stop.

26   See endnote 21.

27   An unidentified bird mentioned by Pliny, sometimes identified with the robin.

28   Presumably listed here as an 'honorary' bird, because of the difficulty of finding a Latin bird's name beginning with v apart from vultur.

29   In the bottom right-hand corner of this illustration, 'Et' is just the teaser for the next page of the text and 'h3' is an instruction to be binder. They are not an integral part of the illustration.

30   In the *Myth of Er* in Plato's *Republic*, Ulysses (Odysseus) is asked to choose a soul for his next incarnation: "There came also the soul of Odysseus having yet to make a choice, and his lot happened to be the

last of them all. Now the recollection of former tolls had disenchanted him of ambition, and he went about for a considerable time in search of the life of a private man who had no cares; he had some difficulty in finding this, which was lying about and had been neglected by everybody else; and when he saw it, he said that he would have done the same had his lot been first instead of last, and that he was delighted to have it" (Benjamin Jowett's translation).

31   i.e. on the blue sea.

32   We do not know to whom this refers.

33   i.e. nonsense or made-up words.

34   See *Judges* 14:6.

35   A reference to Aesop's fable.

36   St. Matthew 3:4: "And the same John had his raiment of camel's hair, and a leathern girdle about his loins; and his meat was locusts and wild honey."

37   See endnote 21.

38   Possibly a reference to the belief that when a cat sits with its back to the fire it is a sign of an impending storm.

39   In Greek mythology, joint ruler of Thebes with his brother Polynices. They quarrelled and eventually killed each other in their struggle for supremacy. According to a poetic tradition that seems to go back to Callimachus, the plume of smoke rising from their funeral pyre divided into two as a token of their enmity.

40   The Greek prisoner of war who fooled the Trojans into bringing the Wooden Horse into their city.

41   As part of his punishment in Tartarus, Tantalus was made to stand in a pool of water underneath a fruit tree with low-hanging branches, but with the fruit always eluding his grasp and the water always receding before he could slake his thirst.

42   Eagles were thought to be capable of looking straight into the Sun.

43   See endnote 26.

44   The word is derived from the Greek, *geranos,* crane, because its pistil resembles a long beak.

45   Small snakes and lizards are eaten by birds such as the African Sacred Ibis.

46   Pope Clement VII is said to have presented a unicorn-horn two cubits long to King Francis I of France at the latter's marriage of his niece, Catherine de' Medici, in Marseilles in October 1533.

47   The Erythræan Sibyl, in Book II of the Carmina Sibyllæ *Erythrææ de Christo Iesu domino n[ost]ro.*
     The relevant part of the text reads:
     Tunc Eromiel,Vriel, Saniel, Azaelque,
     Quæ mala quisque hominum patraverit, ante scientes,

Et tetris animas tenebris caliginis omnes
Iudicio sistent, ad formidabile patris
Magni immortalis solium, etc.

["Then Eromiel [sic], Vriel, Saniel and Azael, knowing beforehand what sins any given man will have committed, will in the horrible darkness of the rising gloom cause all the souls to stand before the terrifying Judgement Seat of the great immortal Father, etc."]

"The Sibylline writings, of unknown origin, were kept at Rome in the Capitol and consulted by the state in times of emergency. They were destroyed in the burning of the Capitol in 82 B.C., and a new collection was made, also burned, in A.D. 405. In the second century B.C., Hellenistic Jews had produced, for propaganda purposes, their own version of the Sibylline Oracles. The Jewish prophecies were freely used by Christian Apologists in the second century, and further oracles from Christian sources were added by the third century. St. Augustine quotes a passage in his City of God (18:23). Other Fathers of the Church, e.g., Theophilus of Antioch and Clement of Alexandria, drew on the Oracles in support of Christ and the Church" (*The Catholic Dictionary*).

48 We do not know why *labrum* should stand for the letter R.

49 So s-a-n-i, to help us remember the name Saniel.

50 So u-r, to help us remember the name *Uriel*, with the bear striking Raymond as the 'action'.

51 i.e. a Moorish girl, dark in complexion.

52 See Appendix.

53 Latin *lituus*, actually a war-trumpet shaped like the number 5.

54 Presumably an error for *quindecim*.

55 An obvious mistake for dextra.

56 Corrected from *regali*.

BV - #0008 - 101120 - C0 - 210/148/8 - PB - 9780853185918